Madam C.J. Walker

ENTREPRENEUR

Muhammad Ali
Maya Angelou
Josephine Baker
George Washington Carver
Ray Charles
Johnnie Cochran
Frederick Douglass
W.E.B. Du Bois
Jamie Foxx
Marcus Garvey
Savion Glover
Alex Haley
Jimi Hendrix
Gregory Hines
Langston Hughes
Jesse Jackson
Scott Joplin
Coretta Scott King
Martin Luther King, Jr.
Spike Lee
Malcolm X
Bob Marley
Thurgood Marshall
Barack Obama
Jesse Owens
Rosa Parks
Colin Powell
Condoleezza Rice
Chris Rock
Clarence Thomas
Sojourner Truth
Harriet Tubman
Nat Turner
Madam C.J. Walker
Booker T. Washington
Oprah Winfrey
Tiger Woods

Black Americans of Achievement
LEGACY EDITION

Madam C.J. Walker

ENTREPRENEUR

A'Lelia Bundles

CHELSEA HOUSE PUBLISHERS

An imprint of Infobase Publishing

Madam C.J. Walker

Chelsea House
An imprint of Infobase Publishing
132 West 31st Street
New York NY 10001

Library of Congress Cataloging-in-Publication Data
Bundles, A'Lelia Perry.
  Madam C.J. Walker / A'Lelia Bundles.
     p. cm. — (Black Americans of achievement, legacy edition)
  Includes bibliographical references and index.
  ISBN 978-1-60413-072-0 (hardcover : acid-free paper) 1. Walker, C. J., Madam, 1867-1919. 2. African American women executives—Biography. 3. Cosmetics industry—United States—History. I. Title. II. Series.

  HD9970.5.C672W353 2008
  338.7'66855092—dc22
  [B]
                          2008008429

Chelsea House books are available at special discounts when purchased in bulk quantities for businesses, associations, institutions, or sales promotions. Please call our Special Sales Department in New York at (212) 967-8800 or (800) 322-8755.

You can find Chelsea House on the World Wide Web at
 http://www.chelseahouse.com

Series design by Keith Trego
Cover design by Keith Trego and Jooyoung An

Printed in the United States of America

Bang ML 10 9 8 7 6 5 4 3 2 1

This book is printed on acid-free paper.

All links and web addresses were checked and verified to be correct at the time of publication. Because of the dynamic nature of the web, some addresses and links may have changed since publication and may no longer be valid.

Contents

"Hit Often and Hit Hard"

"Ladies! Please, may I have your attention? Ladies! Please look towards the camera!" the photographer yelled from atop his ladder as 200 well-dressed women shifted into place on the steps of Philadelphia's Union Baptist Church. All of them were delegates to the first convention of the Madam C.J. Walker Beauty Culturists. They had traveled from nearly every state in America to hear Madam Walker herself advise them on better sales techniques and new hair-care methods. As Walker slipped into the front row for the photograph, she was filled with pride and satisfaction, knowing that her dream to help other black women become economically independent was becoming a reality.

Poor for most of her life, Walker had invented a line of hair-care products when she was 37 years old. Now, 11 years later, in August 1917, she owned and operated her own thriving business, the Madam C.J. Walker Manufacturing Company of Indianapolis, Indiana. Throughout the United States, Central

Proudly wearing their membership badges, delegates to the first annual convention of the Madam C.J. Walker Hair Culturists Union of America assemble in Philadelphia in 1917. Addressing her agents, Walker (front row, center) recommended an assertive approach to selling: "Hit often and hit hard," she urged them.

America, and the Caribbean, she had trained thousands of consultants—almost all of them women—who purchased her products for resale to their customers.

In 1916, she had begun to organize her New York–area agents into the first chapter of the Madam C.J. Walker Benevolent Association, and for the year leading up to her convention, she had traveled to more than a dozen states to urge her sales agents to create local organizations and prepare themselves for the trip to Philadelphia. Her mission was twofold: to show them how to increase their sales and to persuade them that contributing to charitable causes was as important as their personal year-end profits. Through her memberships in other national women's organizations, Walker had observed the power of women's collective action. Now she envisioned something new: an enterprise on a grand scale controlled by economically successful black women with political and civic objectives.

When Walker entered the sanctuary, all the well-coiffed heads turned in her direction. They were, after all, experts in hair care and scalp treatments. Careful attention to their personal appearance was expected.

Walker welcomed her agents, praising them while also reminding them of their responsibility to use their success to advance other women. "I want to show that Walker agents are doing more than making money for themselves," she said. Then she compared the art of sales to a competitive battle. "My advice to every one expecting to go into business is to hit often and hit hard; in other words, strike with all your might."

What's in a Name?

The United States is an ethnically and racially diverse nation, with citizens whose ancestors have come from all over the world. Native Americans—descendants of people who lived in North America before the arrival of Christopher Columbus—were the original Americans. For the past five centuries, other groups from all corners of the world have arrived and made distinctive contributions to American culture.

Today, most Americans who have African ancestors refer to themselves as "African Americans" or "black Americans." Those designations have evolved over time as people of African descent have gained more control over how they are defined in American society. Throughout this book, you will see the words "colored" and "Negro" in quotations because they are the words of the black Americans who used those terms to describe themselves with pride during the early twentieth century. Today, those labels feel old-fashioned and are even considered insulting unless they are used in a historical context or in reference to long-established organizations such as the National Association for the Advancement of Colored People (NAACP), founded in 1909, or the United Negro College Fund (UNCF), founded in 1944.

Born to former slaves on a Louisiana cotton plantation, Sarah Breedlove spent 20 years as a laundress. At the age of 37, however, she invented a hair-care product that made her the wealthiest black woman in the United States.

Knowing that many of the women in the audience had faced enormous obstacles in their lives, Madam Walker told them of her own difficult childhood, her years picking cotton in Louisiana and Mississippi, and the loss of her first husband.

"If I have accomplished anything in life it is because I have been willing to work hard," she said. "There is no royal flower strewn road to success, and if there is I have not found it, for what success I have obtained is the result of many sleepless nights and real hard work."

Certainly other women had developed large companies and created fortunes before hers. Henrietta "Hetty" Green—called the "Witch of Wall Street" because of her miserliness—would die later that year, leaving an estate of $100 million. Annual sales of Lydia Pinkham's patent medicine tonic had reached $300,000 by the time of her death in 1883. Other direct-sales companies had also preceded Madam Walker's. Avon, founded as the California Perfume Company in 1886, counted 10,000 door-to-door sales agents by 1903. The Fuller Brush Company, started the same year as Walker's company, had seen sales of $250,000 by 1917. All had their merits, but none had proposed what Madam Walker was now creating: a national sales force expressly organized around the principles of corporate responsibility, social betterment, and racial justice.

Standing before the convention, Madam Walker, who had been a washerwoman doing other peoples' laundry just 12 years earlier, continued to astonish the saleswomen with stories of her own transformation. A few weeks before the convention, a newspaper reporter had described her as "splendidly poised [wearing] her wealth and honors with ease as if she had [always had them] for all of the years. . . . Madam Walker can hold her own in any gathering of women."

Convened to exchange information and transact business, the agents were also participating in one of the first national conventions strictly devoted to American women's entrepreneurial pursuits. "Nowhere will you find such a large number of successful businesswomen as are among the delegates of this convention," Walker told a reporter.

Throughout the sessions, the delegates shared their personal triumphs. Because of their work as Walker agents, they had been able to purchase new homes, pay for their children's educations, and contribute to their churches. Women who had been paid little more than a few dollars a week as domestic workers now took in two or three or even ten times that much in one day. Margaret Thompson, president of the Philadelphia Union of Walker Hair Culturists, told her colleagues that she had been a five-dollar-per-week servant when she met Madam Walker. "Her income [now] is $250 a week," reported the *Kansas City Star*. Translated into today's dollars, such a salary would equal approximately $4,000 per week, or more than $200,000 per year. In 1917, with the average cost of a new house between $895 and $1,600, Thompson's income—like Walker's even higher income—placed her among the wealthiest Americans. There were scores of success stories like Thompson's because Walker and dozens of other black manufacturers had revolutionized the cosmetics industry by customizing products for black women.

Walker reserved her keynote message—"Women's Duty to Women"—for the final night. From Union Baptist's pulpit she announced proudly that "the art of hair culture" was now being taught at black secondary schools and on college campuses, thus helping to raise the status of those who worked in the industry. She took special pleasure in presenting prizes—$500 in all—to the members who had trained the most new agents and logged the highest sales figures. In an early recycling program, necessitated by wartime restrictions on the use of

IN HER OWN WORDS...

"Perseverance is my motto. It laid the Atlantic cable. It gave us the telegraph, telephone, and wireless. It gave to the world an Abraham Lincoln, and to a race freedom. It gave to the Negro Booker T. Washington and Tuskegee Institute. It made Frederick Douglass the great orator that he was, and it gave to the race Paul Laurence Dunbar and to poetry a new song."

A'Lelia Walker Robinson (seated, front left), Madam Walker's daughter, patronizes the beauty parlor at her namesake Lelia College in New York City. Among the busy salon's attendants is Robinson's adopted daughter, Mae, who stands on the left side of the window at rear.

metals, she awarded $25 to the agent who had returned the largest number of tin containers. It was the women who had contributed the most to their local charities who drew her greatest praise and the largest prizes, however.

A year later, at the second convention, this one in Chicago, Walker continued to emphasize what she called the "benevolent side" of her organization: "I want my agents to feel that their first duty is to humanity." Concerned about the welfare of the black families who were leaving Southern farms for jobs in Northern cities, she urged the delegates to find ways to help people in need. "It is my duty, your duty, to go out in the back alleys and side streets and bring them into your home," she continued, remembering that she had been without a place to live on more than one occasion during her early years as a washerwoman in St. Louis. "Bring them into your clubs and other organizations where they can feel the spirit and catch the inspiration of higher and better living."

In addition to social work, Madam Walker intended to foster political and social activism among her agents. "I shall expect to find my agents taking the lead in every locality not only in operating a successful business, but in every movement in the interest of our colored citizenship," she said.

Just as Walker helped others realize their dreams, she also had set her own goals. In fact, a few months earlier, Walker's attorney, F.B. Ransom, had given her the kind of optimistic annual financial report that let her know that at least some of those goals were within reach. "At the rate you are going," he wrote, "we have now but five years before you will be rated as a millionaire."

Newspaper reporters, fascinated by Walker's wealth, often asked her about her net worth. Replying to a query from a *New York Times* reporter, she said:

> Well, until recently it gave me great pleasure to tell . . . the amount of money I made yearly, thinking it would inspire my hearers. But I found that for so doing some looked upon me as a boastful person who wanted to blow my own horn. . . . I will say, however, that my business last year yielded me an annual income which runs into six figures and I'm going to try to eclipse my 1915 record this year.

A year later, Walker responded to another press inquiry by saying, "I am not a millionaire, but I hope to be someday, not for the money, but because I could do so much to help my race."

2

Motherless Child

Madam C.J. Walker was born with the name Sarah Breedlove on a plantation in Delta, Louisiana, on December 23, 1867. Her parents, Owen and Minerva Anderson Breedlove, and her older siblings, Louvenia, Owen Jr., Alexander, and James, had been born as enslaved people. In 1863, President Abraham Lincoln had signed a document called the Emancipation Proclamation to end the system of American slavery, and Sarah became the first member of her family to be born as a free United States citizen.

Her parents must have hoped that her Christmas-season birth was a sign that her life would be better than theirs. Optimism was not easy for the Breedlove family, though; they made their living growing cotton on Robert Burney's Madison Parish farm. During the summer before Sarah's birth, the cotton crop had been attacked by bollworms—insects that had eaten the plants before they could be harvested. When

Walker was born Sarah Breedlove in this one-room cabin in Delta, Louisiana, in 1867. She was the first member of her family to start life as a free American citizen.

Christmas arrived, the Breedloves had no money to buy presents for Sarah's brothers and sister. In fact, Sarah was the family's special and only gift.

Owen and Minerva, who had been born in the late 1820s, had worked all of their adult lives as field hands. Crops, especially cotton, thrived in the dark, rich soil deposited on the property when the Mississippi River flooded its banks each spring. By 1861, when the Civil War began, Madison Parish had become one of the most prosperous farming areas in the South. Because raising and harvesting cotton required many workers, local planters had purchased large numbers of enslaved people of African ancestry to work for them. Those enslaved human beings, who were not paid for their labor and had no legal rights, outnumbered their white owners by almost 10 to 1 in Madison Parish.

Robert Burney's thousand-acre plantation, one of many that lined this stretch of the Mississippi, included a large house nestled among giant oaks and fragrant magnolias. Known as Grand View, the estate offered a sweeping panorama of the bustling city of Vicksburg, across the river in the state of Mississippi. Steamboats from New Orleans, Memphis, St. Louis, and Louisville arrived in Vicksburg's harbor, delivering passengers and merchandise on the city's busy docks and then picking up cotton to be woven into cloth in factories in New England and Europe. Clanking, puffing trains carried people and products from Vicksburg to the eastern United States, and ferryboats with hooting steam whistles shuttled cargo and travelers between Vicksburg and Delta.

Like much of the South, Delta lay in ruins after the Civil War. Many of its homes, crops, and livestock had been destroyed by Union soldiers who were trying to defeat the Confederate sympathizers who lived there. Although some newly freed slaves left the plantations, Owen and Minerva Breedlove stayed because they had no other way to support themselves.

Delta, Vicksburg, and the Civil War

During the Civil War, Vicksburg's location made it a strategic prize. Controlled by the slavery-supporting Confederacy, the city was surrounded by the Union Army under the command of General Ulysses S. Grant. In 1862, in an attempt to cut communication and supply routes between the Confederacy's eastern and western regions, Grant anchored his gunboats on the riverbanks by the plantation where Sarah's parents lived so he could use the property as a battle-staging area.

In order to divert the Mississippi River from Vicksburg's strategic bluffs, Union engineers directed black men from nearby plantations to dig a canal through the property. The project failed, but after almost a year of Union bombardment, the Confederate forces yielded in Vicksburg on July 4, 1863, marking one of the most important Union victories of the war. Less than two years later, on April 9, 1865, the South surrendered. The war finally was over.

The painting above shows the siege of Vicksburg during the Civil War. In 1878, Sarah Breedlove and her older sister, Louvenia, made a new home in the town. Orphaned and friendless, the two girls made a meager living by washing clothes for wealthy white customers.

Plantation owners, who controlled local governments and state legislatures, often prevented former slaves from buying farmland. After the crop failure of 1867, the federal government ordered black farmers to accept any work they were offered or face arrest. To protect themselves, the Breedloves continued to work for the family that had once owned them, receiving seed and tools in return for a share of the crops they raised.

The sharecropping system almost always worked to the tenants' great disadvantage. They were forced to buy their supplies from the landlord and to process their crops with equipment he owned at high prices that he established. At the end of each season, "croppers" usually owed their employers more than they had earned. For most, the system was not very different from slavery.

BREEDLOVE FAMILY LIFE

Minerva was given no time off to take care of baby Sarah, who had been born in the family's drafty, one-room cabin. The fireplace at one end provided heat and light, but the roof leaked and cold winter air seeped through the wooden shutters past window openings that had no glass.

On Sundays, the Breedloves attended church, where they heard Reverend Curtis Pollard preach about heaven and the Promised Land. He also talked about his experiences as a Louisiana state senator during a brief period called Reconstruction, when black men had temporarily acquired the right to vote in the South. Pollard urged his congregation to speak up for their rights and to educate themselves and their children.

Like many other former slaves who had been prohibited from learning to read and write, the Breedloves craved education for their sons and daughters. For them, literacy was a symbol of freedom. Educating Sarah and her siblings seemed an almost impossible challenge, however: Public schools for black people were rare in Louisiana, and some white people who did not want former slaves to have the same opportunities they enjoyed had burned down schoolhouses and even murdered black teachers and pupils.

Another barrier to education for black plantation families was time. Like other children, Sarah worked alongside her parents in the cotton fields during the planting and harvesting seasons from early spring through late fall. She started out carrying water for the older laborers when she was very young. By the time she was six or seven, she was old enough to drop seeds into the long furrows made by the men and women who pushed the plows.

Sarah also helped her mother with household chores. Saturdays were for laundry, washed in large wooden tubs on the riverbank. From dawn until dusk, Sarah, Louvenia, and Minerva Breedlove used sticks and washboards to beat the soil out of their own clothes and those of their white customers, including the Burney family daughters, who paid them about one dollar per week for the work.

In its own way, washing clothes was as hard as picking cotton. The customers' huge cotton sheets and linen tablecloths were heavy and difficult to handle, especially after being soaked in boiling water and strong lye soap. Still, Sarah loved to listen to her mother and the other women sing while they washed; their harmony and rhythm seemed to make some of the job's drudgery evaporate. At times, when the women's voices blended with the steamboat whistles from the river, Sarah would imagine herself traveling to someplace far away.

Sarah also loved to play with her friend Celeste Hawkins. Sometimes they caught crawfish in the nearby bayous (the creeks that drained into the nearby swamps). In the summer, they went to fish fries and picnics at the Pollard Church, where they sat side by side in the pews. Most of the time, though, she and the other children had to help their parents work.

The combination of endless labor, poor diet, and lack of proper medical care left most of the sharecroppers with little resistance to illness. Cholera, a disease that is caused by unsanitary water and food, and yellow fever, a disease that is carried by infected mosquitoes, stalked the hot, humid communities on the Mississippi River's banks. In 1874, when Sarah was seven years old, her mother died during a cholera epidemic. Within a few months, her father remarried, but he also died soon after. Because no death certificates exist from that time, the exact causes of their deaths are not known.

Sarah missed her parents terribly, but because she and her sister had to survive, there was little patience for her need to grieve. No one seemed to have time to worry about one lonesome, frightened little girl and her younger brother, Solomon, who had been born in 1869. Sarah's older siblings tried to continue farming, but without their parents, they could not manage. Finally, Sarah's brother Alexander moved to Vicksburg to look for work.

Alone on the farm, Sarah, Solomon, and Louvenia found life more difficult than ever. Sarah longed to go to school, but she and her sister spent almost all of their waking moments at their washtubs, trying to make enough money to buy food and pay rent.

In 1878, when Sarah was about to turn 11 years old, yellow fever struck the community again, killing more than 3,000 people in the worst epidemic yet in the Vicksburg region. To make matters worse, the cotton crop also failed that year.

With no work and no money, thousands of people lost their homes. Sarah and Louvenia had no choice but to move across the river. Louvenia hoped she could find work as a washer-

DID YOU KNOW?

With the passage of the Fifteenth Amendment to the U.S. Constitution in 1870, all black men—including those who had been enslaved—were granted the right to vote for the first time in American history. (Black women, along with white women, would not be able to vote in national elections until after the ratification of the Nineteenth Amendment in 1920.) The sudden increase in black voters helped usher in a post–Civil War era called "Reconstruction," when more than 1,500 black men—including U.S. Senators Hiram Revels and Blanche K. Bruce of Mississippi—were elected or appointed to local, state, and national office. By 1880, however, a backlash from whites who opposed black political participation had led to a series of laws that effectively took away the right to vote for most blacks in the Southern United States. This lasted until the passage of the Voting Rights Act of 1965.

Curtis Pollard, the Breedlove's family minister, was a farmer and storekeeper who represented Madison Parish in the Louisiana State Senate from 1868 to 1870 and from 1872 to 1876. In 1879, armed vigilantes forced him to leave the state because he was encouraging other blacks to move to Kansas and Missouri to escape the racism and poor living conditions that they faced in Louisiana.

woman or servant. Many other black Louisiana residents made the same decision, streaming into Vicksburg in a steady tide. At about this time, other black families—who still depended for work on the same plantation owners who had enslaved them—lived in such fear of the Ku Klux Klan and other white terrorist groups that they began to think of ways to leave the South.

Sarah's family minister, Reverend Pollard, encouraged Sarah's older brothers to move to St. Louis, a prosperous town farther north on the Mississippi River. When Alexander, Owen, and James arrived in the Missouri city in 1879 or 1880, they worked as laborers and learned the barbering trade in their spare time. Soon, they had saved enough money to open a barbershop.

When her brothers left, Sarah was even lonelier. After her sister married a man named Jesse Powell, she also felt unsafe. Powell was so cruel to her, in fact, that when she was 14 years old, she ran away to marry a man named Moses McWilliams. (It was not uncommon for girls to marry at an early age in the late 1800s.) Sarah later said she had wanted "to get a home of my own."

Like Sarah, Moses had not been able to go to school, so he worked at jobs that did not require formal education, such as helping to load cotton bales onto boats, repairing the train tracks in Vicksburg, and working in the cotton fields. Sarah picked cotton, too, and continued to launder clothes.

On June 6, 1885, when Sarah was 17, she and Moses had a daughter, whom they named Lelia. Now Sarah was busier than ever, but she was happier than she had been in a very long time. If she worked hard enough, she thought, she could someday make her child's life easier than her own. Soon after Lelia's second birthday, however, Moses died. There is no existing death certificate or obituary, so the cause of his death is not known.

At 20 years old, Sarah was suddenly a widow and a single mother. She was afraid to live with her sister and cruel brother-in-law, so, although she knew she would face many challenges, she began to think about moving to St. Louis to join her brothers. She had heard that there were jobs for laundresses that paid more than she could ever earn in Vicksburg.

All her life, Sarah Breedlove McWilliams had listened to train whistles echoing through the night. She had watched steamboats disappear around the river bend to exciting places. Now she knew it was time to move on. With her toddler strapped to her hip and a boat ticket in her hand, she boarded a northbound riverboat. No matter what the future brought, she told herself, it had to be better than the past.

3

Sarah's Dream

Sarah McWilliams smiled as Lelia skipped off to school. Being able to see her daughter get the education she had never had made all her sacrifices seem worthwhile.

As Lelia disappeared from view, Sarah walked through the hallway of her St. Louis rooming house to the backyard. There, clustered around the rickety porch, stood her wooden wash-tubs. Years later, she remembered the moment: "As I bent over the washboard and looked at my arms buried in the soapsuds, I said to myself, 'What are you going to do when you grow old and your back gets stiff?' This set me to thinking, but with all my thinking, I couldn't see how I, a poor washerwoman, was going to better my condition."

Sarah looked at the baskets of dirty clothes and then sighed and wiped her hands on her apron. She knew her life was better than it had been when she lived in Vicksburg. Still, she could not help feeling discouraged.

When she and her daughter had arrived in St. Louis in 1888, they lived with one of her brothers until they could find their own apartment. Among the city's half-million residents, there were 35,000 African Americans. Swelled by migrants from the Deep South, the black community supported three weekly newspapers and more than 100 businesses.

St. Louis was a far busier place than Vicksburg. The downtown sidewalks were filled with white and black Missouri natives, transplanted Easterners, and European immigrants who hurried past the gas-powered streetlights. Fashionably dressed ladies in expensive horse-drawn carriages looked out their windows as shabbily dressed peddlers pushed wagons filled with fresh vegetables, ice, and coal. By the 1890s, the city would be home to the headquarters of Anheuser-Busch, the nation's largest brewery; W.R. Warner and Company, its most important drug manufacturer; and Liggett & Myers, its biggest tobacco factory.

Along the St. Louis riverfront and near the train station, noisy, dimly lit saloons and cafés attracted nightly crowds of gamblers and hustlers. Ragtime, the infectious, syncopated piano music that seemed to come from the heart of black St. Louis, poured from dance halls and bars. People tapped their feet to the rhythms of popular tunes such as "Ragtime Millionaire," with lyrics that captured the hopes, humor, and heartaches of the community: "I'm afraid I may die of money disease/Don't bother a minute about what those white folks care/I'm a ragtime millionaire!"

Sarah could not imagine herself a millionaire, but she had no trouble finding work as a washerwoman. Difficult as the job was, it was better than working as a house servant, which seemed to be the primary option for a black woman with no formal education. At least washing clothes in her own home meant that she could keep an eye on Lelia.

It broke Sarah's heart every time she thought about her first year in St. Louis, when she had been separated from her child

while she worked as a live-in maid. Because she was sometimes homeless and because there were no daycare centers
for working mothers, she had been forced to leave Lelia at
the St. Louis Colored Orphans Home for part of every week.
The women who had founded the home, however, were very
kind to Sarah and Lelia. One, who was a member of St. Paul
African Methodist Episcopal (AME) Church, invited Sarah to
join the church. Established in 1840, St. Paul was the first St.
Louis church planned, built, and financed by African Americans. Defying the pre–Civil War laws that made it a crime to
teach black people to read and write, St. Paul had sponsored a
secret school for its members. After the war, the church helped
former slaves find jobs so that they could rent homes and pay
for clothes and food.

The women of the church were friendly and generous to
Sarah. One particularly helpful person was Jessie Robinson, an
elementary school teacher, who could see that Sarah wanted to
improve her life. With Jessie's encouragement, Sarah began to
view herself differently. In fact, she began to believe that she
did not have to remain an illiterate washerwoman. She also
listened to Jessie's advice to leave her husband, John Davis,
an alcoholic with a violent temper whom she had married in
1894.

For now, Sarah focused on caring for her daughter. She also
took pride in her work as she scrubbed stains from dirty col-
lars and pressed the delicate lace and ruffles of her customers'
clothes with an iron she heated on a stove over an open flame.
As she pulled the clean and neatly folded clothes in a wagon
across the Eads Bridge—which spanned the Mississippi River
between St. Louis, Missouri, and East St. Louis, Illinois—she
walked with dignity, knowing she had done an excellent job.
She often marveled at the skill of the engineers who had built
this massive brick-and-steel structure. There must be a way,
she thought, to build a bridge to prosperity for herself and
Lelia. In her prayers, she asked God to help her.

She also knew she would have to help herself. Although she was paid very little for her work, she began to save a few pennies each week. By the time Lelia completed eighth grade, Sarah was able to afford $7.85 per month for her daughter's tuition and room and board at Knoxville College, a small black institution in Tennessee with classes for high school students.

With Lelia away at school, Sarah used her free time to become more active in her church, volunteering her time as a member of the Mite Missionary Society, the St. Paul organization that assisted needy members of the community. Years later, a newspaper article described one of Sarah's first activities for the group: "She read in the [St. Louis] *Post-Dispatch* . . . of an aged colored man with a blind sister and an invalid wife depending on him for support. Without acquaintance of any kind with the family, she went among friends in the behalf of the distressed people, succeeding in collecting $3.60 which she gave to them." The newspaper also reported that, because she "felt it was her duty to do even more," she arranged to collect groceries and an additional $7.50. At a time when a loaf of bread cost five cents and a quart of milk cost six cents, this was a very helpful gift.

Among the missionary society's members were a number of prominent, well-educated black women. Through them, Sarah encountered a new world and a new way of looking at her own circumstances. She was impressed with their stylish clothes and polite manners and inspired by their ability to organize themselves and to become community leaders.

Sarah was also awed by the black leaders who came to St. Louis for the 1904 World's Fair. Although many of the public facilities at the fair were racially segregated, several famous black people, like poet Paul Laurence Dunbar and scholar and political activist W.E.B. Du Bois, attended. Even Tuskegee Institute Principal Booker T. Washington, who was considered the most influential black leader of his time, delivered two important speeches there.

A 1910 photograph of then—43-year-old Walker shows a serene, fashionably attired woman, strikingly different from the neat but shabbily dressed laundress of earlier days.

During the fair, 200 delegates of the National Association of Colored Women (NACW), held sessions for their biannual convention at Sarah's church. These women, who represented 15,000 members from 31 states, had helped found orphanages, retirement homes, kindergartens, and recovery clinics for tuberculosis patients. Some of the local women were the same ones who had helped Sarah and Lelia when they had first arrived in St. Louis.

Because the fair officials refused to hire black workers for anything other than menial jobs, the NACW members voted to boycott the fair and canceled the visit they had been planning for several months. Instead, they met at St. Paul AME Church to continue their business proceedings. NACW President Margaret Murray Washington—the wife of Booker T. Washington—led them in discussions about lynching, segregated trains, and other important issues.

Like many of the delegates, Sarah admired Mrs. Washington's poise and confidence, but she also felt a little self-conscious about her own threadbare dresses. She was beginning to see the link between inner attitude and outward appearance. How she felt about herself inside was reflected in the way she carried herself.

Sarah could not afford expensive dresses and shoes, but she always wore clean, carefully ironed clothing, the better to advertise her skills as a laundress. No matter how she dressed, though, she was embarrassed by her hair: She had split ends and bald spots that showed her infected and inflamed scalp.

At a time when most American women washed their hair only once a month—because they did not have indoor plumbing and electricity—many women shared Sarah's hair and scalp problems. Sometimes poor nutrition, stress, and illness caused hair loss, and sometimes it was the result of hair-care treatments with harmful chemicals and harsh ingredients. Many black women were targeted by advertisements for products like Queen Pomade, La Creole Hair Restorer, Kinkilla, and Ford's Original Ozonized Ox Marrow that crowded the pages of black newspapers. Often, these ointments with the strange and funny names did more harm than good.

The manufacturer of Thomas's Magic Hair Grower claimed that its product would "cleanse the scalp of dandruff, stop it from falling, and make it grow even on bald spots." Because many black people criticized hair straightening as behavior that imitated white people, Thomas's ads stressed that its product was "NOT A STRAIGHTENER." Although they did not want to copy white females, few black women in the cities wore the traditional hairstyles and elaborate ornaments of their African foremothers. Many yearned for long hair and more versatility in caring for their hair.

Sarah was desperate for a solution to grow her hair and heal her scalp. She tried several products, including the Poro Company's Wonderful Hair Grower, made by another black St. Louis woman named Annie Malone. Soon, Sarah was working as a sales agent for Malone, but it did not take long for her to realize that she had her own ideas about how to operate a business. She believed that she could improve Malone's products and sales methods.

Because Malone already had a number of agents in St. Louis and because Lelia was at school in Tennessee, Sarah decided to leave Missouri to test the market for hair-care products in other places. Still working for Malone, she packed her belongings and moved to Denver, where her widowed sister-in-law, Lucy Breedlove, now lived. All of Sarah's brothers had died within the past few years, and her sister lived in Arkansas, so Sarah no longer had close family members in St. Louis. She believed that Lucy and Lucy's four daughters could help her get established in a new city.

In July 1905, Sarah stepped off the train at Denver's Union Depot with $1.50, which was equal to about a day's pay for her work as a laundress. Colorado's mountains and wide blue skies astonished her, and she found the city's crisp, dry air a welcome change from the steamy heat of St. Louis. Along the city's wide boulevards, she saw cattlemen, silver miners, land speculators, and frontiersmen jockeying for their share of the riches and adventure promised by the West.

Colorado's entire state population was only slightly larger than the city population of St. Louis. When Sarah arrived, fewer than 10,000 black people lived there, and even in Denver, where slavery had never been legalized, blacks still faced discrimination. At the same time, some black residents had persevered and started their own businesses. A few had become quite prosperous, running hotels, investing in silver mines, and buying real estate.

Settling into the Mile High City (as Denver is known because of its elevation above sea level), Sarah rented an attic room, joined the Shorter Chapel African Methodist Episcopal Church with her sister-in-law, and found a job as a cook. According to family legend, her employer was E.L. Scholtz, a

Making Soap and Hair-Care Products

In colonial America, soap was made most often by boiling animal fat with wood ash lye, an alkaline liquid that was created by straining very hot water through ashes that resulted from burning wood or plant leaves. A much finer type of soap made from olive, coconut, and palm oils rather than animal fat had become preferable for bathing and washing hair by the early twentieth century, when Madam Walker began to make her hair-care products.

At a time when most Americans did not have indoor bathrooms, Madam Walker emphasized the importance of frequent shampooing as the essential first step to healing scalp disease and maintaining good grooming.

To make her product, Walker first measured her ingredients: olive oil, coconut oil, and lye, and then boiled them in a large metal pot on her stove. While she slowly stirred the mixture by hand with a large wooden spoon, she also added scents like violet and lavender to make the shampoo more appealing. After about an hour, she poured the mixture into molds to cool. The next day, after the soap had hardened, she transferred it to a round tin container with a label that showed her photograph and the words "Madam Walker's Vegetable Shampoo."

When her factory opened in Indianapolis in 1910, she was able to hire other women to manufacture much larger quantities of her shampoo as well as the hair and scalp ointments that were sold to customers in the United States, the Caribbean, Central and South America, Europe, and Africa.

Canadian-born druggist who owned the largest, best-equipped pharmacy west of Chicago. His drugstore mixed doctors' prescriptions as well as home remedies and medicinal tonics.

Sarah is said to have consulted Scholtz about ingredients for the hair preparations she was creating to replace the products she bought from Annie Malone. She spent her evenings working on her formulas and testing them on herself and her nieces. Finally, she came up with three products that met her requirements. She called them Wonderful Hair Grower, Glossine, and Vegetable Shampoo.

In early 1906, Sarah informed friends that, with divine help, she had learned how to make the mixture she wanted. She later told a reporter:

> God answered my prayer, for one night I had a dream, and in that dream a big black man appeared to me and told me what to mix up for my hair. Some of the remedy was grown in Africa, but I sent for it, mixed it, put it on my scalp, and in a few weeks my hair was coming in faster than it had ever fallen out. I tried it on my friends; it helped them. I made up my mind I would begin to sell it.

Before long, Sarah had saved enough money to be able to afford to leave her job as a cook. To pay her rent, she took in laundry two days each week. The rest of the time she spent developing her products and selling them door to door.

Others could see that Sarah had a special talent for promoting her goods. One of her bright marketing ideas was to give free treatments but to charge for the products. Once her customers saw the results, they were eager to buy. After washing a woman's hair with her Vegetable Shampoo, she applied her Wonderful Hair Grower. This product contained sulfur, a medication that could cure dandruff and other conditions that caused hair loss. To complete the demonstration, Sarah brushed a light oil through her customer's hair and then

BEFORE USING

Walker used photographs of herself to illustrate the effects of her products, as shown in the advertisement above. A customer who looked at a "before" picture and then at the saleswoman herself was inevitably surprised. When Sarah explained that her long, well-groomed tresses were the result of her treatments, the customer was usually convinced to place an order.

combed it with a metal comb that she had heated on a stove. This procedure softened the tight curls that characterized the hair of many people of African descent.

Denver's black women began to buy her wares with enthusiasm. At first, she used all her profits for raw materials and advertising. Her ads in the *Colorado Statesman*, a black Denver newspaper, generated mail orders, and her personal sales trips to nearby towns produced encouraging results.

Sarah's best advertisement, however, was herself. A customer who looked at a "before" picture and then at the saleswoman herself couldn't help but be surprised. When Sarah unpinned her hair and explained that her long, well-groomed tresses were the result of her treatments, the customer was almost sure to place an order.

After her move, Sarah had stayed in touch with Charles Joseph Walker, a St. Louis friend and newspaper sales agent. She wrote to him about her increasing business. After providing a steady stream of advice by mail, Walker, known to all as C.J., arrived in Denver in late 1905. A few weeks later, on January 4, 1906, Sarah and Walker were married at a friend's home.

Because he was familiar with newspaper promotion campaigns, Walker helped his new wife expand her mail-order business. To give a special mystique to her business, Sarah began to call herself "Madam C.J. Walker" and renamed her product "Madam Walker's Wonderful Hair Grower." The title made her customers think of Paris, the world's fashion and beauty capital, where married women used the title "Madame."

In the United States of the early 1900s, women had fewer guaranteed legal rights than men. They could not vote in federal elections, and, in most states, they could not own houses or land unless their fathers or husbands gave them permission. Because of racial discrimination, black women had even fewer rights and opportunities.

By the time the Walkers' business was bringing in $10 per week (or about $230 in today's dollars), Sarah's husband decided it had reached its full potential. Sarah, though, believed that if more women knew about her Wonderful Hair Grower, they would buy it. With this in mind, she made plans for an extended sales trip to other states.

Her husband and some of her friends predicted that she would not be able to earn enough to pay her travel expenses. She left anyway, setting out in September 1906 for what would become a year and a half of visits to nine states, including Oklahoma, Louisiana, Mississippi, and New York. Although Mr. Walker was not entirely confident about her plan, he agreed to accompany her. Within a few months, they were making weekly sales of $35—equal to a little more than $800 in today's dollars—more than 4 times the salary of the average white American male factory worker and 20 times that of the average black woman worker.

By this time, Lelia, who now was 21 years old, had left Knoxville College. She moved to Denver to help run the mail-order business while her mother and stepfather traveled. Elegantly dressed and nearly six feet tall, Lelia brought a creative flair to

Hair and Race

Hairdressing and barbering have a long tradition in the African-American community. In the days of slavery, black men and women often tended to the hair of the slave owners as well as to their own. In the late 1900s, many of the most elegant barbershops in America were owned by black men. Centuries earlier in Africa, hairstyles with as many variations as the hundreds of tribes that inhabited the continent denoted age and gender as well as marital and social status. African women spent hours, even days, creating intricate, beautiful braids into which they wove shells, beads, and other ornaments. Some women wore wigs made of human and animal hair or plant fibers. Others dyed their hair with soot or colored it with clay. However they styled their hair, African women did so with a sense of ancient tradition and pride.

By the twentieth century in America, the legacy of slavery had severely damaged the self-image of many black people. Because the system of slavery had created a hierarchy of power that favored whites as superior based on their physical appearance and racial traits, black or brown skin had come to signify bondage, and unstraightened hair and African facial features were deemed inferior. All of the models who appeared in magazines and newspapers during the 1890s, when Madam Walker was losing her hair, were women of European descent with long, straight hair. Those European standards of beauty had become the ideal and caused many people to falsely believe that kinky and curly African hair was not attractive. In reality, all hair could be beautiful if cared for properly.

Acutely aware of the debate about racial identity and pride, Walker sought to create a look that was truly African American and that also addressed women's concerns about their appearance. Her solution was to urge women to concentrate on grooming and on emphasizing their own good points without trying to imitate whites.

her sales pitches. Even with the help of her Aunt Lucy and her four cousins—Anjetta, Thirsapen, Mattie, and Gladis—however, Lelia could barely keep up with the orders her mother mailed to her every week.

While Madam Walker was on the road, she realized that she could expand her operation even more if she trained other women to become her sales agents. By spring of 1908, she had recruited dozens of representatives and brought her company's monthly income to $400 (nearly $52,000 in today's dollars). Now, with a growing mail-order operation, she decided to move her company to a part of the country where she would have access to a larger population of black women, who were the customers most interested in her products.

After a visit to Pittsburgh, Walker selected the Pennsylvania city as her new base of operations. A thriving industrial and banking center, Pittsburgh boasted an extensive transportation system and a rapidly increasing black population.

In Pittsburgh, Walker rented an office on Wylie Avenue, the main street of the city's black community, where there were 45 churches, 22 doctor's offices, 5 law offices, and dozens of businesses, including tailor shops, restaurants, funeral homes, and pharmacies. The area was home to a number of prosperous black families, but most of the city's black residents worked in service jobs or as laborers.

Although the bulk of Pittsburgh's mining and manufacturing jobs went to newly arrived European immigrants, waves of black Southerners were moving to the city, eager to take whatever work they could find. Businesswoman Walker saw the influx of black residents as a source of new agents and customers.

In the summer of 1908, Lelia joined her mother and stepfather in Pittsburgh. Together, the women opened a beauty parlor and a training school for Walker agents, which they called the Lelia College of Beauty Culture. A graduate of the school would be known as a "hair culturist," they decided,

In the summer of 1908, Lelia and Walker opened a beauty parlor and a training school for Walker agents, which they called the Lelia College of Beauty Culture. A graduate of the school would be known as a "hair culturist." A diploma from the school is shown above.

because she prepared and conditioned her customers' scalps to grow or "cultivate" the hair.

Word of the new school spread quickly. Applications came from housekeepers, office cleaners, laundresses, and even schoolteachers, all women whose needs and dreams Walker understood well. Over the next two years, Lelia College graduated dozens of hair culturists who now had opportunities they had never had before. In a letter to Walker, one graduate said, "You have opened up a trade for hundreds of colored women to make an honest and profitable living where they make as much in one week as a month's salary would bring from any other position that a colored woman can secure."

In 1910, the *Pennsylvania Negro Business Directory* ran a feature story about Walker, calling her "one of the most successful businesswomen of the race in this community." The article included a photograph of Walker, showing her as a woman whose appearance had changed dramatically in only a few years. Posed with her hands clasped behind her back and her long hair pinned neatly on top of her head, Walker looked confident and serene. Her high-necked, floor-length dress resembled the expensive clothing of her former laundry customers more than the patched dresses she had worn during her days as a laundress.

As she became more financially prosperous, Walker was invited to events hosted by the city's prominent black citizens, including clergymen and the women who headed community and church organizations. People she had once admired from a distance now were admiring her and all the things she had been able to accomplish.

4

Gearing Up

In Pittsburgh, Madam Walker quickly turned her beauty school, mail-order, and door-to-door operations into an even more profitable business. After about a year, she began to realize that Pittsburgh lacked some of the assets she needed to take her business to the next level. When she visited Indianapolis, Indiana, in early 1910, she decided she had found the right city for her permanent national headquarters. Indianapolis, called the "Crossroads of America," had extensive highway and train networks that created a perfect transportation system for Walker's mail-order operation. Although Indianapolis lacked a major waterway, it had become the country's largest inland manufacturing center because of its access to eight major railway lines. More than one million freight cars passed through the city every year, and hundreds of national and regional passenger trains arrived each day.

In an era before large numbers of Americans began to move to California and other western states, Indiana was right at the center of the most populous areas of the nation. As a result of this key location, scores of large manufacturing and industrial companies also were located there. During the first two decades of the twentieth century, Indianapolis also was one of the major centers of America's new automobile industry. In 1909, the year after Henry Ford introduced his Model T car, the city built the Indianapolis Motor Speedway. Originally designed to test-drive cars, the Speedway became a racecourse after the first Indy 500 race in 1911.

Walker also was attracted by the city's thriving black business community. During her first visit to the Hoosier capital, Walker met publisher George L. Knox, whose newspaper, *The Indianapolis Freeman*, was one of the nation's most widely read black weeklies. Knox had prospered as a businessman and told Walker of the opportunities that awaited an ambitious entrepreneur in Indianapolis. He urged her to settle there and backed his argument for Indianapolis by telling Walker his own story.

Born a slave in 1841, Knox had arrived in Indianapolis in 1864. Eventually, he opened his own 10-chair barbershop in one of the city's most prestigious hotels and used his access to wealthy white customers to advance himself economically and politically. By the late 1890s, he had become the city's leading black businessman and the state's most powerful black politician.

His experience, Knox told Walker, was not unique. The black community's main thoroughfares, Indiana Avenue and North West Street, were lined with cafés, offices, restaurants, and salons. Knox pointed to H.L. Sanders, a former hotel waiter who had become America's most prosperous black uniform manufacturer. At the time of Walker's visit, Sanders, his wife, and their 25 employees were producing work clothes for hospital aides, hotel workers, janitors, and domestic employees in Indiana, Ohio, Kentucky, Illinois, and Michigan.

Walker (second row, second from the left) reunites with a group of old friends outside of the Indianapolis YMCA, the building she helped endow in 1913. Standing in the front row (second from left) is George Knox; fourth from the right in the back row is Robert Lee Brokenburr, the attorney who signed on as Walker's part-time adviser in 1911.

After hearing about Indianapolis's assets and observing the civic pride of Knox and other Indianapolis boosters, Walker made up her mind. "I was so impressed with [Indianapolis] and the cordial welcome extended," she said later, "that I decided to make this city my home."

Leaving her 24-year-old daughter—who had recently married a Pittsburgh hotel worker named John Robinson—in charge of the company's Pittsburgh operations, Walker moved to Indianapolis with her husband in February 1910. Shortly after she arrived, Knox introduced her to a young black attorney named Robert Lee Brokenburr. Born in 1886 in Virginia,

Brokenburr had attended Hampton Institute—Booker T. Washington's alma mater—and graduated from the Howard University School of Law in 1909.

At Knox's recommendation, Walker hired Brokenburr as a part-time legal adviser. In September 1911, he filed articles of incorporation for the Madam C.J. Walker Manufacturing Company, a corporation that would "manufacture and sell a hair growing, beautifying and scalp disease-curing preparation and clean scalps with the same."

During her travels, Walker had met another young attorney, Freeman Briley Ransom. Born in Grenada, Mississippi, in 1882, Ransom had studied at Columbia University Law School, moved to Indianapolis in 1911, and set up his own law office. In exchange for room and board in Walker's home, he gave her legal advice.

As her travel schedule became heavier, Walker realized that she needed someone with legal skills to oversee her company's day-to-day operations. After much discussion, she persuaded Ransom to sign on as her full-time attorney and general manager. Brokenburr, who continued his private law practice, agreed to become the company's assistant manager.

Brokenburr and Ransom sometimes disagreed on political and philosophical issues, but they respected each other and worked well as a business team. Like many young black professionals of the time, they shared a belief that they were pioneers with opportunities that their parents and grandparents had not had. Walker knew that she could count on them to protect her business interests while she was traveling.

With her daily operations now firmly under control, she began to focus her attention on her company's future. Everywhere she went, she recruited new Walker agents and employees. On one Southern sales trip, she met Alice Kelly, a teacher at Kentucky's Eckstein Norton Institute, then a boarding school for black children. Impressed with the younger woman's decisive, assertive manner, Walker offered her a job in Indianapolis.

Walker stands on the porch of her house in Indianapolis. When her business outgrew Pittsburgh, Walker sought a new location to take her business to the next level. She chose Indianapolis, called the "Crossroads of America," which had extensive highway and train networks that could serve as a transportation system for Walker's mail-order operation.

Kelly learned quickly, and Walker soon asked her to become the supervisor of her Indianapolis factory. She was so impressed with Kelly, in fact, that she entrusted her with the company's secret hair-growing formula, until then known only by Walker and her daughter. Walker also hired one of Kelly's former students, Violet Davis Reynolds, as her private secretary.

The more successful Walker became, the more she wanted to improve her communications skills. Acutely aware of her lack of formal education, she sought Kelly's advice on social etiquette, penmanship, public speaking, letter writing, and literature. Acting as both traveling companion and tutor, Kelly often joined Walker on sales trips.

Walker continued her lessons at home and in her Indianapolis office. Each morning, as she sat at her desk reading the newspapers, she asked Reynolds or bookkeepers Lucy Flint and Marie Overstreet to look up unfamiliar words in the dictionary. As she educated herself, she educated her staff. She knew that her company's continued success depended on knowledgeable employees.

Walker's many sales trips, as well as her extensive advertising campaigns in the nation's black newspapers, brought daily product orders from all over the United States. Within a year of her arrival in Indianapolis, Walker announced a set of impressive statistics: Her company now had 950 agents nationwide and a monthly income of $1,000, or almost $22,000 in today's dollars. She put her profits back into the business, expanding her factory, purchasing a second building, and hiring more employees. Located in the heart of the city's black community, the Walker Company employed neighborhood women who had never had such a promising chance to improve their lives. After an intensive training program in hair and beauty culture, the graduates served a stream of eager customers, giving them scalp treatments, restyling their hair, and administering manicures and massages.

Always serious about her work, Walker also found time for cultural activities and entertainment. She became a patron of the arts, hosting concerts and poetry readings. She gradually filled her home with beautiful furniture and oil paintings commissioned from talented young black artists. In her parlor stood a mahogany baby grand piano, along with a custom-made phonograph and a harp, both covered with gold leaf accents. Walker often spent her evenings listening to recorded music, reading in her library, or playing Flinch, a popular card game of the day, with friends.

Fascinated by the era's grand theaters and silent films, Walker was an eager movie enthusiast. On many afternoons, Alice Kelly and Violet Reynolds would ride with her to the movie houses nearby in downtown Indianapolis. On one particular trip, however, Walker's expectation of a pleasant hour at the cinema turned to disappointment and anger.

Arriving at the Isis Theatre, she gave the ticket seller a dime, standard admission price at the time. The agent pushed the coin back across the counter. The price, she said, was now 25 cents. Responding to Walker's frown, the salesperson explained that the admission price had gone up—but only for "colored persons."

Furious, Walker went home and instructed attorney Ransom to sue the theater. He immediately filed a complaint, accusing the Isis of practicing "unwarranted discrimination

Madam Walker Theatre Center Today

Designated a National Historic Landmark in 1991, the Madam Walker Theatre Center—a four-story, block-long flatiron building—opened in December 1927. For more than four decades, the Indianapolis building housed the corporate headquarters and factory of the Madam C.J. Walker Manufacturing Company, as well as a beauty school, a beauty salon, a drugstore, a restaurant, professional offices, a ballroom, and a 1,500-seat theater. From the 1920s through the 1960s, the Walker Theatre featured first-run movies and an array of black performers—from blues queen Mamie Smith to jazz greats Dinah Washington and Wes Montgomery. Today, the building and its African–art deco theater are home to a thriving cultural arts and education center that has showcased premier African-American music and performance art—from tap dancer Savion Glover and jazz pianist Ramsey Lewis to lyric soprano Paula Dione Ingram and singers Patti LaBelle and Kenneth "Babyface" Edmonds.

When Walker encountered discrimination at the cinema in Indianapolis, she resolved to make a movie theater part of her new office building, which also included a larger factory, a beauty salon, a drug store, and corporate offices. Today, the building (shown here in the 1950s) is home to a thriving cultural arts and education center.

because of the color of this plaintiff" and asking for a $100 fine. (No further records of the suit exist, possibly because the theater settled the complaint out of court.)

Walker, who rarely did anything in half measures, next began to make plans for a new office building with a larger factory, a beauty salon, a drug store, and corporate offices. Now she was even more motivated to push forward. Completed some years later, the Walker Building would cover an entire block in downtown Indianapolis—and would include one of the city's most beautifully designed movie theaters.

Few members of Indianapolis's black population—about 10 percent of the city's 233,650 people in 1919—escaped encounters with discrimination. Walker was no exception, but her wealth and prominence gave her access to some areas closed to most African Americans. The city's bankers, for example, treated her cordially—as they would treat any customer who deposited large sums of money each year. Recognizing her efficiently run company as a solid investment, Indianapolis banks were willing to lend money to Madam Walker so she could expand her business.

Walker also received a warm welcome in the city's department stores and automobile showrooms, where many other black customers were not encouraged to shop. One white jeweler, grateful for Walker's purchases of silver and diamonds, made it a point to walk outside and greet her whenever he saw her car arrive.

In the midst of her success, Walker began to have serious disagreements with her husband about control of the company and plans for its expansion. Their business differences spilled over into their personal life, finally resulting in a decision to end the marriage. Sarah Walker filed for divorce in late 1912, but she would retain her husband's name for the rest of her life.

5

"My Own Factory
on My Own Ground"

After her divorce, Walker devoted even more time to her company. As she watched revenues rise from $1,000 every month to $1,000 every week, she could measure the results of her efforts. Meanwhile, her daughter—now known as A'Lelia Walker Robinson—was beginning to expand the company's East Coast operation into New York City.

On one of her visits to Indianapolis, A'Lelia met 13-year-old Mae Bryant. Mae was a frequent visitor to the home of her grandmother, Samira Thomas, a few doors away from the Walker office and factory. Mae often ran errands for the women in the Walker beauty salon. Madam Walker occasionally demonstrated treatments on Mae, who made an ideal model because she had very long, thick, healthy hair. In fact, her braids were so long they came down to her hips.

Mae's mother, Etta Bryant, whose ancestors were African, European, and Native American, was descended from a North

Long-haired Mae Bryant was 13 years old when A'Lelia Walker Robinson hired her as a model for Walker products. Charmed by the bright, attractive young woman, Robinson eventually adopted her, providing Madam Walker with her only grandchild.

Carolina family whose members had been free people of color. Two of her great-great-grandfathers had been soldiers in the Revolutionary War and had owned land at a time when most black people in America were enslaved. In the 1830s, her grandparents had moved to Indiana to seek better opportunities. They also felt pressured to leave North Carolina because some of the state's white citizens wanted to take away the civil rights of residents of African descent. The family joined other relatives in Indiana who had purchased land and started a community called the "Roberts Settlement." When Mae's father, Perry Bryant, died in 1909, her mother was left with no savings and eight young children to rear. The family was struggling so hard that Etta was relieved to have the extra money Mae could earn working as a model and helper for the Walker women.

As Madam Walker and A'Lelia came to know Mae better, they realized she was a smart child who might benefit from the advantages their wealth could provide. Soon, Mae was spending more and more time with the Walkers on their sales trips to other cities. Eventually, A'Lelia, who had no children of her own, asked Etta Bryant to let her legally adopt Mae. She assured Etta that she would give Mae a good education and allow her to keep in touch with her brothers and sisters and large extended family in Indiana. Aware that A'Lelia Robinson could provide Mae with more advantages than she herself could, Bryant consented to the adoption.

When A'Lelia returned to Pittsburgh, Mae went with her. When Madam Walker stopped there on sales trips, she often had Mae join her so she could teach her more about the business. With her adopted granddaughter, Walker spent much of the summer of 1912 along the East Coast and in the upper Southern states, giving lectures and promoting her business at conventions held by black religious, fraternal, and civic organizations.

In July, Walker arrived in Chicago for the National Negro Business League convention poised to persuade the group's founder, Booker T. Washington, to let her address the more than 200 black American entrepreneurs who had journeyed to this Illinois city. Earlier that year, when Walker had visited the Tuskegee Institute, the Alabama vocational school Washington had helped found in 1881, he had been polite but less than enthusiastic about her presence on his campus. This time, Walker was determined to win him over.

At the convention's opening assembly, Walker listened closely to one success story after another. Massachusetts real estate broker Watt Terry, for example, told the audience how he had started his career by purchasing a single house. After selling it at a profit, he invested his money and eventually acquired 50 houses and 2 apartment buildings now worth half a million dollars.

The accounts of Terry and his fellow businessmen would have been striking under any circumstances. What made them truly remarkable, however, was their race. Half a century earlier, almost all black Americans had been enslaved. In 1860, one out of every seven Americans had been the property of another.

Walker found herself especially intrigued by the words of Anthony Overton, who described his Overton Hygienic

Black Entrepreneurs

When the Civil War—and slavery—ended in 1865, most African Americans who had done agricultural work lacked the kind of math, accounting, industrial, and manufacturing skills they needed to become entrepreneurs. Most of those who tried to start their own businesses found it impossible to borrow money from the large banks, which were owned by whites. Those who did manage to offer products or services found few white customers willing to purchase their goods. Nevertheless, a number of enterprising black merchants had established small but profitable operations such as barbershops, catering firms, sail-making shops, funeral homes, pharmacies, and dry-goods stores.

By 1900, when Booker T. Washington, himself a former slave, founded the National Negro Business League to help promote black commerce, close to 20,000 black-owned businesses existed in the United States. By the time of the 1912 convention, that number had doubled. Despite these impressive figures, though, most black Americans were still quite poor. A black businessman was rare, a black businesswoman even rarer.

Manufacturing Company of Chicago as "the largest Negro manufacturing enterprise in the United States." From the sale of its products, which included cosmetics, face powder, and baking powder, the Illinois firm had earned more than $117,000 during the previous year. This was just the kind of success Walker hoped to achieve with her company.

When Overton finished speaking, Washington asked for questions from the audience. George Knox, Madam Walker's Indianapolis friend and publisher of *The Indianapolis Freeman*, stood up. "I arise to ask this convention for a few minutes of its time to hear a remarkable woman," he said. "She is Madam Walker, the manufacturer of hair goods and preparations."

Acting as though Knox had not spoken, Washington recognized another audience member. Walker was frustrated and suspected from previous correspondence with Washington that he looked down on her line of work: the manufacture and sale of hair treatments for black women. Nevertheless, she resolved that the convention would hear from her, even if she had to speak up without Washington's permission. At the next morning's session, she sat patiently through a long lecture by an Indianapolis banker and then another by a Texas banker. As each man returned to his seat, she tried to get Washington's attention, but he seemed to avoid looking in her direction.

Finally, while the audience was applauding Washington's remarks about the Texas banker, Walker sprang to her feet. "Surely you are not going to shut the door in my face," she said firmly. "I feel that I am in a business that is a credit to the womanhood of our race. I started in business seven years ago with only $1.50."

The audience looked at the 44-year-old businesswoman with curiosity. Who was this determined speaker with the satiny, cocoa-colored skin and the beautifully groomed hair?

"I am a woman who came from the cotton fields of the South," said Walker. "I was promoted from there to the washtub." These words caused some to snicker, because many people looked down on women who washed other people's laundry. "Then I was promoted to the kitchen, and from there *I promoted myself* into the business of manufacturing hair goods and preparations," continued Walker in a strong voice. "I have built my own factory on my own ground." Now, respect replaced the audience's laughter.

"My object in life is not simply to make money for myself or to spend it on myself," Walker said. "I love to use a part of what I make in trying to help others."

Walker finished her speech and returned to her seat as rousing applause filled the auditorium. When the crowd began to quiet down, Knox took the floor. "I arise to attest all that this good woman has said concerning her business," he declared.

That evening, Walker's unscheduled speech was the talk of the convention. Delegates clustered around her after dinner, eager to learn more about this newcomer with the expensive clothes, dignified manner, and firm beliefs.

Responding to her colleagues' questions, Walker said she believed that more black women should strike out on their own. "The girls and women of our race," she asserted, "must not be afraid to take hold of business endeavor and . . . wring success out of a number of business opportunities that lie at their very doors."

A few of the men disagreed. Their wives, they said, should stay at home and take care of their families and do housework. Walker had no time or patience to debate that issue. Many black American women had no choice but to work outside their homes; those who were unmarried, widowed, or single parents had to support themselves. Many of the married women worked because the racial discrimination that excluded their husbands from skilled labor occupations and office jobs meant that the men could find only low-paying jobs.

Black women earned less than any other working group in America. Ninety percent of African Americans lived in the rural South in 1910, and many of the black women who worked were farmers and sharecroppers who did as much physical labor as men. A few who lived in cities managed to become schoolteachers or nurses. Some had opened beauty parlors or seamstress shops, but most took jobs as maids, cooks, or laundresses. In the first decade of the twentieth century, very few black women earned more than $1.50 per week (or about $32 in today's dollars), whereas the average unskilled white worker earned about $11 weekly.

Walker told the conference delegates about the way her program had already helped many black women. After learning the Walker system of hair care, either at one of her schools or through a correspondence course, a Walker agent could open a shop in her own home to treat customers and sell Walker products. Her agents, Walker said, enjoyed both personal independence and an increased income, allowing them to buy homes and send their children to school.

By 1912, Walker had trained more than 1,000 women. They were, she told her listeners, making $5, $10, and even $15 or more per day. "I have made it possible," she said proudly, "for many colored women to abandon the washtub for more pleasant and profitable occupation." As the Chicago convention ended, delegates continued to talk about Walker and her innovative business practices. Even Washington, who had snubbed her at first, would soon show that this dynamic, energetic woman had impressed him.

Several months later, Washington attended the dedication of the new Young Men's Christian Association (YMCA) building that had been constructed in Indianapolis for black boys and men. Although it was a segregated facility and less well equipped than the state-of-the-art local white YMCA, it was a huge improvement over the rickety structure it had replaced.

Sharing the stage with keynote speaker Washington were a number of prominent local black entrepreneurs, including Madam C.J. Walker. She had stunned YMCA building-fund

Friends of Indianapolis's new black YMCA assemble on the building's steps in 1913. In the front row are (from left) *Freeman* publisher George Knox, Madam C.J. Walker, Booker T. Washington, *Indianapolis World* publisher Alex Manning, and YMCA executives R.W. Bullock and Thomas Taylor. Standing at the rear are Walker's longtime business associate, F.B. Ransom (left), and her physician, Colonel Joseph Ward.

officials by contributing $1,000, the largest sum ever received from any individual black donor, male or female.

Washington told the dedication ceremony's 1,200 guests that the new YMCA would improve the lives of the city's young men. "This building," he said, "should mean less crime, less drink, less gambling, less association with bad characters," and should make its users "more industrious, more ambitious, more economical." Walker was very pleased when, at the end of his speech, Washington paid tribute to her generosity and her work, which he called "a business we should all be proud of."

A few weeks later in Philadelphia at the NNBL convention, Washington—who had enjoyed Walker's hospitality as her houseguest during his recent visit to Indianapolis—invited Walker to be a featured speaker. As she walked to the podium, he said, "I now take pleasure in introducing to the convention one of the most progressive and successful businesswomen of our race—Madam C.J. Walker."

"If the association can save our boys," Walker said as she got to the heart of her message, "our girls will be saved. And that is what I am interested in. Someday I would like to see a colored girls association started."

When Walker concluded her remarks, Washington thanked her for "all she has done for our race." Then he added a compliment that surely made Walker smile. "You talk about what the men are doing in a business way," he said. "Why, if we don't watch out, the women will excel us!"

That was exactly what Madam C.J. Walker intended to do.

6

"Don't Sit Down and Wait"

Madam Walker's mind always seemed to be racing with ideas for improving her business. She had learned that a few dollars spent on an advertising brochure could result in thousands of dollars in sales and that a positive newspaper article could reach hundreds of potential customers. She was convinced, though, that her personal appearances in towns and cities across America generated the most interest and new business.

As she planned her travel schedule for the summer of 1912, she happily anticipated several weeks on the road. After only a few days in Indianapolis, she left for Hampton, Virginia, to attend the biennial conference of the National Association of Colored Women, the same group of women she had observed at her St. Louis church during the 1904 World's Fair. Among the other NACW delegates was Mary McLeod Bethune, the 37-year-old founder of the Daytona Normal and Industrial Institute for Negro Girls. Determined to bring schooling to a Florida area that offered black children no education at all, Bethune had opened her tiny institute eight years earlier. By 1912, the school was accepting boys as well as girls and had changed its name to the Daytona Educational and Industrial Training School.

Impressed by Bethune and her work with children, Walker volunteered to lead a fund-raising effort for the school's benefit. The two women's mutual respect led to a lifelong friendship.

From Virginia, Walker continued her nonstop travels, speaking and demonstrating her products at black churches, fraternal lodges, and public halls. By train and by car, she visited hundreds of communities, sometimes joined by her daughter, her nieces, or her granddaughter. The young women helped with the demonstrations and other chores, like handing out brochures and registering new Walker agents.

Because telephones were very rare at the time and computers and e-mail did not exist, Walker depended on letters for communicating with her staff in Indianapolis. From the road, she wrote daily notes to her staff and to Ransom, instructing them on company operations and describing her sales efforts. Back in Indianapolis, each day's mail delivery brought hundreds of dollars worth of orders from Walker and her agents. In a May 1913 letter to Walker, Ransom said, "Your business is increasing here every day. I think you are the money making wonder of the age."

Ransom, who considered himself Walker's financial watchdog, sometimes gently scolded her for what he regarded as extravagance. In one letter to him, Walker said, "Am writing to let you know I have given a check for $1,381.50 to the Cadillac Motor Co. Won't you see to it that the check is cashed? . . . I guess you think I am crazy, but I had a chance to get just what A'Lelia wanted in a car. . . ." Ransom's response was, "No, I don't think you crazy, but think you very hard on your bank account. I take pleasure in the fact that there can hardly be anything else for you to buy, ha, ha!!"

Convinced that the Walker Company needed a base in New York City, A'Lelia persuaded her mother to buy a house there. For its location, A'Lelia selected Harlem, the northern Manhattan neighborhood then just starting to attract large numbers of black residents. By late in the spring of 1913, A'Lelia had purchased a town house on 136th Street, near Lenox Avenue. She opened a beauty salon and another Lelia College of Beauty Culture on the first floor and in the basement, and she had living quarters upstairs.

Arriving in New York with Alice Kelly in the midst of the renovations, Walker was extremely pleased with what she saw. "In regards to this house," she wrote to Ransom, "you will agree with A'Lelia when she said that it would be [a] monument for us both. . . . The Hair Parlor beats anything I have seen anywhere, even in the best Hair Parlors of the whites. There is nothing to equal it, not even on Fifth Avenue." Walker was not alone in her admiration for her daughter's handiwork. The *Chicago Defender,* a nationally distributed black newspaper, called the establishment "the most completely equipped and beautiful hair parlor that members of our Race ever had access to."

Confident that the office was in good hands with A'Lelia, Walker spent the rest of that summer and early fall traveling in her seven-passenger Cole touring car to several East Coast cities, including Philadelphia, Atlantic City, Baltimore, and Washington, D.C.

In the nation's capital, Walker gave speeches in 10 churches, among them the First Baptist Church in Georgetown and the downtown Metropolitan AME Church. In her lecture "The Negro Woman in Business," she told audiences how she had achieved success through hard work and careful planning and then urged other women to follow her example and establish their own businesses.

"Now I realize that in the so-called higher walks of life, many were prone to look down upon 'hair dressers,' as they

Convinced that the Walker Company needed a base in New York City, A'Lelia persuaded her mother to buy a house there. For its location, she suggested Harlem, and by late spring of 1913, A'Lelia had purchased a town house (shown above) on 136th Street, near Lenox Avenue.

called us," she told her listeners. "They didn't have a very high opinion of our calling, so I had to go down and dignify this work, so much so that many of the best women of our race are now engaged in this line of business," she added proudly.

The more Walker traveled and the more new people she encountered, the more possibilities she saw. On her way home

After A'Lelia purchased the Harlem town house, she opened a beauty salon and another Lelia College of Beauty Culture on the first floor and in the basement. Her living quarters were upstairs. Shown above is the first-floor salon and its luxurious furnishings.

from Washington, D.C., she began to think about expanding her business overseas. She knew that people of African descent—potential customers who could use hair-care products designed for their hair texture—lived all over the world. Central America, the Caribbean, and South America had heavily concentrated black populations. Developing an international market seemed to be a logical next step.

After researching the area by consulting with associates who had traveled and lived there, Walker sailed for the West Indies in November 1913. Five days later, she arrived in Kingston,

Jamaica, with her touring car and enough products and supplies to last three months. With Jamaica as her base, she visited Cuba, Haiti, Costa Rica, and the Panama Canal Zone, demonstrating the Walker hair-care method just as she had throughout the United States—and just as they had in the United States, women flocked to see her, to buy her goods, and to sign on as her agents.

When she returned to Indianapolis in January, Walker found her office and factory employees working to fill the product orders. To celebrate her success, she hired local singer and entertainer Noble Sissle—who later would become a Broadway star in New York—and invited several relatives and friends to a spring dance at the Knights of Pythias Hall. Walker also frequently entertained at home, where her guests tasted hors d'oeuvres and sipped punch served from a sterling silver punch bowl.

The following summer, Walker made a whirlwind tour of the northeastern United States to promote her products. As usual, audiences received her with enthusiasm. "My lecture Monday night was a grand success," she wrote to business manager Ransom from one New England town. "The house was packed. The people applauded so I hardly had time to talk. . . . I have been entertained two and three times a day ever since I've been here. Haven't had a day or evening to myself."

Walker made increasingly frequent trips to New York and liked the city better with each visit. Harlem, which buzzed with conversations of politics, business, music, and theater, gave her renewed energy. She found herself welcomed by the black community's most prominent residents: composer and conductor James Reese Europe, who had performed at Carnegie Hall; *New York Age* publisher Fred Moore; Shakespearean actor Richard B. Harrison; and realtor Philip A. Peyton, whose Afro-American Realty Company had helped open Harlem to black tenants and homeowners. By 1915, Walker was spending almost as much time in New York as in Indianapolis. She began to consider moving east to be closer to her daughter and granddaughter.

During the final weeks of summer, Walker was traveling again, this time to previously untapped markets in Utah, Montana, Oregon, Washington, and California. Always thinking of ways to create excitement for her audiences, she had added a new dimension to her lectures: a slide show featuring illustrations of her hair-care system along with photographs of black leaders and schools and businesses founded by African Americans.

Shortly after her return to her Indianapolis headquarters, Walker announced that she had decided to live in New York City. Her manufacturing operation, she said, would remain in Indiana under the management of Ransom, Kelly, and Brokenburr. Walker's friends were sad to hear that she planned to leave and tried to persuade her to reconsider. Ransom, ever concerned about fiscal matters, protested vigorously. He insisted that the move would be too expensive and that it would interfere with Walker's ability to run the business. Walker, though, had made up her mind. She wanted to live in

IN HER OWN WORDS...

At the 1914 convention of the National Negro Business League, held in Muskogee, Oklahoma, Walker said:

> I am not merely satisfied in making money for myself, for I am endeavoring to provide employment for hundreds of the women of my race. I had little or no opportunity when I started out in life, having been left an orphan. . . . I had to make my own living and my own opportunity! But I made it! That is why I want to say to every Negro woman present, don't sit down and wait for the opportunities to come. . . . Get up and make them!

New York, the center of progressive thinking and activity for African Americans.

As she prepared for her farewell party, she reminisced about her arrival in Indianapolis six years earlier. Few people had heard of her then, but now she was known as "the foremost businesswoman of the race."

Less than a decade earlier, Walker had been struggling to meet her own expenses. Now people recognized her for her contributions to orphanages, schools, churches, civic organizations, and other charities. As she headed downstairs to join her guests, she heard the unmistakable melody of "Auld Lang Syne": "Should auld acquaintance be forgot . . ."

HELPING OTHER WOMEN SUCCEED

At the root of Madam C.J. Walker's astonishing success lay her high-quality products, her gift for inspiring and leading others, her ability to build a strong sales force, and her self-confidence. That sense of assurance, which grew even more as she became economically independent, touched other women, who wanted to follow her example.

"Lots of people tell me I've been lucky," Walker often told her sales agents. "I don't call it luck. I had to work mighty hard. It takes faith in yourself and in God, and it takes push and pluck and honest dealing to succeed."

From her own experience, Walker knew that many women could succeed if just given the chance and the training. She hired women at all levels of her company, from factory workers to national sales agents. By 1916, 20,000 agents were selling her products in the United States, Central America, and the Caribbean. These women often wrote letters to tell Walker how she had changed their lives. Florida agent Lizzie Bryant told her, "I have all I can do at home and don't have to go out and work for white people in kitchens and factories."

At the time, black women workers in the Northern United States earned an average weekly salary of $10; their Southern

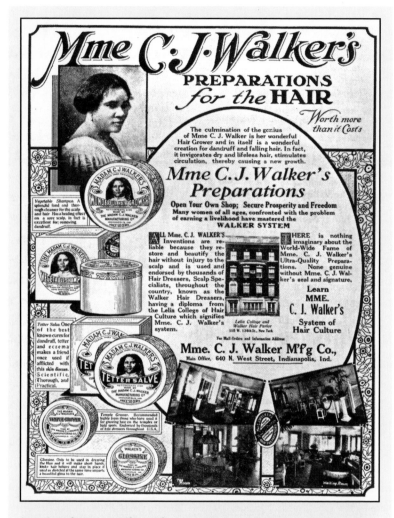

In advertisements like this one, Madam Walker used her own photograph, allowing customers to see that she, like many of them, was a brown-skinned woman with the facial features and hair texture of someone with African ancestry. In this way, Walker assured girls and women that all textures of hair could be beautiful if properly cared for.

counterparts in 1916 brought home less than $2 per week (or $38 in today's dollars). Walker-trained women fared much better: "A diploma from Lelia College of Hair Culture is a Passport to Prosperity," assured one advertisement. In a 1913 letter to the company, Mrs. Williams James of Columbus, Ohio, said, "We have been able to purchase a home and over-meet our obligations. Before I started out as an agent in Madam Walker's employ, I made the regular working woman's wage, but at this writing I average $23 a week."

"Open your own shop," read a typical Walker ad. "Secure prosperity and freedom. Many women of all ages, confronted with the problem of earning a livelihood, have mastered the Walker System." In an era of wildly exaggerated advertising, the Walker claims were rather modest. They were also truthful. Almost any woman with drive, determination, and creativity could pass the Walker course, whether she took it by mail; at one of the Lelia Colleges in Pittsburgh, New York, or Indianapolis; or from Walker and her traveling instructors.

In late 1916, Walker began to offer her courses to black colleges and trade schools throughout the South. Many schools accepted her plan, which included the free installation of a small campus beauty salon and training facility. Educator Mary McLeod Bethune, who had become Madam Walker's friend at the 1912 NACW convention, welcomed the Walker course for her students at the Daytona Educational and Industrial Training School. "For the past four years my girls and myself have been using your Wonderful Hair Grower," she wrote to Walker in March 1917. "We have proven it to be very beneficial indeed and would be glad to place it in our school as a course of study."

Walker was concerned about the controversy over whether black women straightened their hair with heated metal hair-care implements or wore it naturally kinky and curly. Her objective was to encourage them to strive for clean, healthy hair—whether it was straightened or natural—and to feel proud of themselves. "Right here let me correct the erroneous impression held by some that I claim to straighten the hair," she once told a reporter. "I want the great masses of my people to take a greater pride in their personal appearance and to give their hair proper attention. . . . And I dare say that in the next ten years it will be a rare thing to see a kinky head of hair and it will not be straight either." By that, Walker was assuring girls and women that all textures of hair could be beautiful if properly cleaned, groomed, and cared for.

Walker considered the ritual of her system as important as any resulting hairstyle. She taught her agents to create an atmosphere that allowed their customers to feel pampered. The personal attention gave women a chance to focus on themselves, boosting their confidence and sense of self-worth in the process. For black women, who rarely found themselves valued in American society at that time, the psychological lift was enormous.

Walker agents learned a philosophy of inner and outer beauty. "To be beautiful," asserted the Walker Beauty School textbook, "does not refer alone to the arrangement of the hair, the perfection of the complexion, or to the beauty of the form. . . . To be beautiful, one must combine these qualities with a beautiful mind and soul; a beautiful character. Physical and mental cleanliness, together with [good health] are essential to attain loveliness."

Most manufacturers of black hair-care and cosmetic products featured idealized white women or biracial black women with very light complexions and naturally straight or wavy hair in their ads. Not Walker. She used her own photograph on her products and in her advertisements, allowing customers to see that she, like many of them, was a brown-skinned woman with the facial features and hair texture of someone with African ancestry. The ads seemed to say, "Buy Walker's products and look like Walker. Look like Walker, and you too may achieve her success."

Walker pushed that notion of prosperity among her beauty culturists as well as her customers. In one letter about new promotional material that Ransom was writing to send to her agents, she suggested, "In those circulars I wish you would use the words 'our' and 'we' instead of 'I' and 'my.'" Her leadership style was to build a team rather than to place herself above her employees.

The Walker agents' handbook stressed the importance of keeping accurate financial records, clean beauty salons, and a neat personal appearance. "See that your hair always looks well . . . to interest others," the handbook counseled.

Walker also continued to encourage her agents to be leaders in their communities and to contribute part of their profits to charity. Genuinely interested in aiding other black people, she knew that her own well-publicized philanthropy increased sales. Every time she donated money to a school or church, the newspapers covered the story. By doing a good deed, she was able to link the purchase of Walker products with the well-being of black Americans, who still were denied jobs and education because of the color of their skin. In many ways, Walker began to realize that her business and financial success had become a means to a greater end of helping others.

7

"We Should Protest"

In 1916, when Walker arrived in Harlem, a wave of Southern black and West Indian migrants was reaching its peak in New York and other Northern cities. Sparking the migration was the promise of good jobs and a better life.

Coming after two years of boll weevil invasions, the summer floods of 1915 had made already intolerable living conditions even worse for poor Southerners, both black and white. Jobless, homeless, and hungry, many black Southerners were forced to look for work outside the region. The battles of World War I had begun to damage and destroy many cities in Europe, and the difficulties of wartime travel had drastically curtailed the number of European immigrants coming to the United States. To fill positions in Northern factories, employment agents swept through the South, ready to hire anyone willing to work. Although black workers usually were offered the lowest-paying jobs, they felt fortunate to have the chance to make more money than they could in Mississippi, Alabama, Georgia, South Carolina, North Carolina, Kentucky, or Tennessee.

The hundreds of thousands of black Americans who fled the South between 1915 and 1920 were also escaping segregation, racial violence, and lynching. As the *Chicago Defender*, a black newspaper, put it, "To die from the bite of frost is far more glorious than at the hands of a mob."

Of all the Northern cities, New York, and specifically Harlem—which had become the cultural and intellectual mecca of black America—seemed the most exciting destination. The residents of Harlem established trends and influenced styles in music, literature, art, and fashion that were adopted by blacks and whites throughout the world.

In the realm of cosmetics and skin care, two recent European immigrants, Elizabeth Arden and Helena Rubinstein, dictated the standards for white American women. For black women in New York, the queen of beauty culture was Madam C.J. Walker, whose success mirrored the spirit of possibility that many sensed in Harlem. The spacious four-story brick-and-limestone town house, which she now shared with A'Lelia and Mae, had become a focal point for Harlem's elite, who competed for invitations to Walker's dinner parties and cultural evenings. Well-known African-American musicians often entertained her guests.

The Harlem branch of the Lelia College of Beauty Culture, under A'Lelia's supervision, now graduated 20 Walker hair culturists every six weeks. Mae had also learned to teach the Walker system and assisted with the management of the beauty salon.

As Mae's eighteenth birthday approached, A'Lelia and Madam Walker decided that it was time to broaden her education, as they had promised Etta Bryant, and to prepare her to take on more responsibility for the Walker company. In September 1916, A'Lelia enrolled Mae at Spelman Seminary in Atlanta, Georgia, the nation's first all-female black college.

Meanwhile, the family business continued to prosper. In October, while Walker was traveling, her factory shipping clerk, Raymond Turner, wrote to her from Indianapolis: "We have more mail than anyone at the post office. . . . Miss Kelly sent a big shipping order to Mrs. Robinson of 13,234 Grower, 3,904 Glossine and 1,002 shampoos." In Pittsburgh alone, the Walker operation was bringing in $2,000 per week from sales of popular products such as Wonderful Hair Grower and Vegetable Shampoo.

Madam Walker, the company's energetic chief executive, had continued to act as its principal sales agent, traveling from state to state, making speeches, organizing demonstrations, and taking product orders. By the fall of 1916, however, 48-year-old Walker was ready to turn some of this exhausting travel over to others. She knew she could count on Alice Kelly and a few handpicked, carefully trained executives to do the job. Departing for a swing through the South in September, Walker declared that it would be her last major sales trip. Clearly she was enjoying herself, though. After visiting Salisbury, North Carolina, she wrote happily, "I was very much flattered at the splendid turnout to hear my lecture. Both black and white came. They were all loud in their praise." In a note from Savannah, Georgia, she said, "My trip here was a howling success in that I have been able to get before thousands of people and all the big guns have shown me the greatest courtesies and kindness." From Mississippi, she wrote, "I surely made a hit in Natchez and am sure we'll get some good business from there."

When Walker reached Washington, Georgia, she found the townspeople suffering from a disappointing cotton-harvesting season that had put them in debt. "I'm having quite a deal of success here with the work," she wrote to Ransom, "but I've found so many poor people who cannot raise $25.00 that I've decided to let them have the trade for $10.00. . . . I put them on their honor to pay whenever they can."

Walker sits at the wheel of her brand-new Model T Ford. Though Walker enjoyed driving, she often traveled with her chauffeur. The other women in the car are Walker's niece Anjetta Breedlove, bookkeeper Lucy Flint, and factory forewoman Alice Kelly.

From Georgia, Walker went to her childhood home in Louisiana. "Delta was honored Sunday," reported the local paper, "by a visit of the richest Negro woman in the world, [Madam] C.J. Walker." Walker received a warm welcome from Anna Burney Long, owner of the plantation where Walker had been born and the daughter of the man who had owned Walker's parents, Minerva and Owen Breedlove, when they were enslaved. After chatting with Long, Walker walked down the dusty road to the cabin where she and her family had lived.

She stood outside, remembering her parents and her difficult childhood. No one, she reflected, could have dreamed that little Sarah Breedlove would grow up to be one of the wealthiest businesswomen in America. Walker could not help but enjoy a sense of triumph, knowing that she had been blessed with such good fortune.

Still, something was bothering her. All her life, she had possessed the kind of energy and drive that allowed her to help herself. With success, she had transferred some of that energy to helping others. Lately, however, she had started to feel tired, with an occasional overwhelming sense of fatigue. Although her spirit was always willing, sometimes her body was not. Walker's doctors had warned her of high blood pressure and insisted that she cut back on eating fried and fatty foods. Although they knew she would not listen, they also asked her to cut back on her business activities.

Still on the road in mid-November, Walker had a life and death scare as she traveled through Clarksdale, Mississippi. She wrote to Ransom the next day:

> After leaving the church, we had to cross a railroad track. As soon as the car we were in got on the track we heard a man yelling, "Get out of the way!" We looked around in time to see a freight train backing down on us, not a bell ringing or anything. The chauffeur in the nick of time put on more gas and shot forward. The train all but grazed the back of the car in which we were riding. I haven't been myself since.

The doctor who examined Walker after the near catastrophe advised her to take a long vacation. "I think instead of coming home, I will go to Hot Springs where I can really get rest and quietude," she wrote to Ransom. "The doctor advises me to take not less than six weeks rest." At the bottom of Walker's letter, her traveling companion typed a postscript: "Dear Mr. Ransom," it said. "Thank goodness we have finally persuaded Mme. Walker to take that much needed rest. Today the doctor told me she was on the verge of a nervous breakdown. . . . You keep telling her after she gets to Hot Springs to remain there for the six weeks."

Walker obediently settled into a health spa in Hot Springs, Arkansas, but she found it hard to relax. Within days of her arrival, she wrote to Ransom again: "I promise you I am going to let all business alone and look strictly after my health except little things which I am going to write to you about now. Ha. Ha."

Located on the edge of central Arkansas's Ouachita National Forest, Hot Springs featured dozens of wells bubbling with steaming, mineral-rich water that was said to cure a variety of ailments. Wealthy visitors from all over the United States "took the waters" at Hot Springs and relaxed in the area's elegant, European-style bathhouses. Her associates thought that the tense, overtired Walker was in the right place to relax—if she could manage to sit still for a few weeks.

Hoping to keep her at Hot Springs, A'Lelia and factory supervisor Alice Kelly joined her there for the Christmas holidays. The three women spent much of their time at the bathhouse owned by the Knights of Pythias, a black fraternal organization. Every morning, Walker soaked in hot mineral water as she sipped a soothing herbal tea and then showered in a spray of brisk water jets. Afterward, wrapped in hot towels, she rested in a darkened room until it was time for her daily massage.

Surprising her family and friends, Walker stayed at Hot Springs until February. Then, full of renewed energy, she set off on a two-month trip through Texas and Louisiana that brought a record-breaking surge of business.

In April 1917, soon after Walker returned to New York, the United States entered World War I. The conflict triggered a debate in Harlem and throughout black America: Should black men enlist to fight? Many said yes, sure that their country would reward their loyalty with respect. Others, however, thought that the fight for civil rights was more important than defending America in a military conflict. Instead, they believed that their country should grant them full rights as citizens before asking them to risk their lives overseas.

The second group had very real reason for concern. Many white Americans felt threatened by black Americans' increasingly outspoken call for equal political and civil rights. Once Booker T. Washington had died, other more militant voices started to call for black citizens to have the same legal rights as all Americans. Some white Americans agreed, but many had become even more adamant in their opposition to this notion. Racism had been on the rise since the end of the post–Civil War Reconstruction period and had reached terrifying proportions by the beginning of the twentieth century's second decade.

Despite social and economic inequality and the federal government's seeming lack of concern for the welfare of its black constituents, a number of prominent black leaders believed that black Americans should cooperate in the nation's war effort. They believed that such a demonstration of loyalty would prove to whites that blacks had an equal stake in the nation's welfare and therefore deserved equal rights as citizens.

Among this group of committed people were two leaders of the National Association for the Advancement of Colored People (NAACP): W.E.B. Du Bois, editor of the organization's magazine, *The Crisis*, and Field Secretary James Weldon Johnson. Both men advised blacks to join with white Americans in support of the war effort.

Strongly approving of the Du Bois–Johnson approach, Walker lent her name—by now widely known in both the black and the white communities—to the government's efforts to recruit black soldiers. She threw herself into the cause with her usual vigor. Visiting training camps around the country, she offered moral support and encouraged young black soldiers to be patriotic.

Remembering Walker's visit to his military base, one sergeant later wrote her a letter from Europe. "We all remember you," he said. "We have often spoken of you and of the words of consolation which you gave us at Camp Sherman, Ohio, on the eve of our departure. Those words have stayed with the boys longer than any spoken by anyone that I have known or heard of."

Despite the sacrifices of black soldiers and others who supported America in the war, major race riots swept several American cities during the summer of 1917. The worst of these deadly uprisings took place in East St. Louis, Illinois, where mobs murdered 39 blacks, seriously injured hundreds of others, and drove thousands of families from their homes. In some cases, whites torched the homes of blacks and then shot them as they tried to escape. Black children, women, and men were drowned, burned, and beaten. Some white police-men refused to arrest the attackers.

After the riot, a profound sense of outrage united the nation's black citizens. Adding to their anger and grief was the knowledge that thousands of young black men had dem-onstrated their support for America by joining the armed forces—knowledge particularly galling to those who, like Walker, had urged them to volunteer to fight for their country. In Harlem, Walker joined other leading citizens to design a way to express the community's pain and to demand an end to mob violence. The result was the Negro Silent Protest Parade, staged in Manhattan on July 28, 1917.

Shortly after noon on that Saturday, about 10,000 black New Yorkers began a somber, purposeful march down Fifth Avenue. Block after block, the only sound that broke the city's hush was the dirge-like roll of muffled drums and the muted thunder of marching feet. More than 20,000 spectators, who were as silent as the marchers, lined the avenue.

In the parade, dark-suited men carried banners and signs that protested Jim Crow laws, mob violence, and disenfran-chisement. "Treat Us So That We May Love Our Country," read one banner. The female marchers, who included a number of Walker agents, wore white dresses and escorted rows of neatly dressed children.

Marchers fill Manhattan's Fifth Avenue during the Negro Silent Protest Parade in 1917. Sparked by a murderous attack on blacks in East St. Louis, Illinois, and organized by Walker and her associates, the parade drew 10,000 participants and twice as many spectators.

Heartened by the public show of solidarity, Walker and her colleagues pressed on, hoping that they could persuade national officials to make lynching a federal crime. Like murder—which it was—lynching was a state crime rather than a federal crime. Civil libertarians hoped for a special federal law to ban the barbaric practice, because the Southern states in which it was most often committed almost never prosecuted the mostly white lynchers, who hanged, shot, and burned their mostly black victims.

The Harlem group drafted a petition and requested a meeting with President Woodrow Wilson to discuss the issue. In addition to Walker, James Weldon Johnson, and W.E.B. Du Bois, the petition signers included Reverend Adam Clayton

Powell Sr. of Harlem's Abyssinian Baptist Church, Harlem realtor John E. Nail, and *New York Age* publisher Fred Moore. Although the petition was respectful and courteous in tone, it made its point unmistakably clear.

"Mobs have harried and murdered colored citizens time and time again with impunity, culminating in the latest atrocity at East St. Louis," said the text in part. "We believe that this spirit of lawlessness is doing untold injury to our country. . . . We ask, therefore, that lynching and mob violence be made a national crime punishable by the laws of the United States."

In response to the Harlem delegates' request, Wilson's secretary, Joseph Tumulty, promised them an appointment with the president. On August 1, four days after the Silent Parade, Walker and her colleagues arrived at the White House. As scheduled, Tumulty appeared in the executive waiting room at

Woodrow Wilson and Racism

By the time Democratic President Woodrow Wilson was elected in 1912, much of the political progress blacks had made after the Civil War had been reversed. Campaigning for office, Wilson had promised black leaders that he would treat black Americans with "absolute fairness," that he would encourage their employment in federal agencies, and that he would establish the National Race Commission to study the health, education, and economic status of blacks.

After his election, Wilson—the first Southern-born president to occupy the White House since the Civil War—went back on his promise by reintroducing racial segregation to public buildings and restrooms in the nation's capital and forcing many blacks from their jobs in federal agencies. Wilson appeared to be sympathetic to an antiblack backlash and also had hosted a private White House screening of *The Birth of a Nation*. This 1915 movie celebrated the Ku Klux Klan, a terrorist organization founded after the Civil War to reestablish white supremacy in the South. Klan "Knights" roamed the countryside, burning large crosses and kidnapping, beating, and murdering blacks and Catholics. Inspired by these hooded nightriders, American racists embarked on an epidemic of lynchings: Between 1885 and 1916, nearly 3,000 blacks met violent deaths at the hands of white mobs.

noon exactly. He greeted the group cordially and then said that the president was too busy signing a farm bill to see them.

Walker and her friends had not come to Washington expecting miracles. They knew Wilson's views on racial matters reflected the attitudes of the Old South. They also knew that he had hosted a private showing at the White House of *The Birth of a Nation*, a movie that portrayed black people in an unflattering, inaccurate, and stereotypical manner. Still, the Harlemites had hoped that the president would understand the urgency of their message and that he would keep his appointment with them. Extremely disappointed, they presented their petition to Tumulty and left the White House.

The group spent the remainder of the day visiting senators and congressmen who were sympathetic to their cause. Congress eventually appointed a committee to investigate the East St. Louis riot and introduced two new antilynching bills. Like all previous legislation designed to punish racially motivated mob violence, these bills were defeated by Southern white legislators who opposed equal legal rights for black Americans.

Despite the government's failure to condemn lynching, Walker believed that there might be political leverage in staying involved, so she continued to urge other black Americans to support the war effort. At her 1917 convention for Walker agents, she advised the group "to remain loyal to our homes, our country, and our flag." At the same time, however, she maintained that blacks should keep fighting for justice and equal rights.

"This is the greatest country under the sun," she said. "But we must not let our love of country, our patriotic loyalty cause us to abate one whit in our protest against wrong and injustice. We should protest until the American sense of justice is so aroused that such affairs as the East St. Louis riot be forever impossible."

Just as Walker had encouraged her agents to become community leaders, she now encouraged them to become political lobbyists who worked to influence lawmakers to support their causes and interests. After listening to Walker's 1917 speech, the agents voted to send a telegram to Wilson declaring their patriotism while also demanding their rights as full citizens. The telegram read:

> Honored Sir: . . . Knowing that no people in all the world are more loyal and patriotic than the Colored people of America, we respectfully submit to you this our protest against the continuation of such wrongs and injustices [as the East St. Louis race riot] and we further respectfully urge that you as President of these United States use your great influence that congress enact the necessary laws to prevent a recurrence of such disgraceful affairs.

With that gesture, the association had become what perhaps no other currently existing group could claim: American women entrepreneurs who organized to use their money and numbers to assert their political will.

HER DREAM OF DREAMS

Deeply involved in her business and increasingly committed to political activities, Walker still found time to design and build her dream house. In late 1916, she had bought a large piece of land in Irvington-on-Hudson, a wealthy community just north of New York City that was home to industrialists John D. Rockefeller and Jay Gould. Her purchase of the property, which perched on the eastern bank of the broad Hudson River, had originally caused concern among Irvington's white residents. The *New York Times* reported that

> On [Walker's] first visits to inspect her property, the villagers, noting her color, were frankly puzzled, but when it became known that she was the owner . . . they could only gasp in astonishment. "Impossible!" they exclaimed. "No woman of her race could own such a place." To say that the

village, when the report was verified, was surprised, would be putting it mildly. "Does she really intend to live there, or is she building it as a speculation?" the people asked.

The *Chicago Defender*, on the other hand, regarded the situation with some amusement. Walker's purchase of the Irvington estate, said the black newspaper, had "created a furor, for one of the Race was invading the sacred domains of New York's most sacred aristocracy."

In September 1917, with construction well underway, Walker invited her friend Ida B. Wells-Barnett, a journalist and antilynching crusader, to join her for a visit to see the property. The businesswoman and the activist first had met several years earlier, just as Walker was starting her business. "I was one of the skeptics that paid little heed to her predictions as to what she was going to do," Wells-Barnett recalled years later. "To see her phenomenal rise made me take pride anew in Negro womanhood."

Wells-Barnett was properly impressed with the grand marble entryway that was taking shape. Walker showed her the sweeping terraces and balustrades along the back of the house, as well as the area where the sunken Italian garden was planned, but Wells-Barnett was puzzled by the size of the mansion. "I asked her on one occasion what on earth she would do with a thirty room house," she noted in her autobiography, *Crusade for Justice.* "She said, 'I want plenty of room in which to entertain my friends. I have worked so hard all my life that I would like to rest.'"

Rest, of course, was exactly what Walker usually managed to avoid. Several weeks after Wells-Barnett's visit, the entrepreneur's blood pressure shot up. Her physician sent her to a medical clinic in Battle Creek, Michigan. There, doctors made an announcement she did not want to hear: If she had any interest in remaining alive, she "must give little or no attention again to business or heavy social activities."

8

"A Conference of Interest to the Race"

No matter what her doctors said, Walker was so passionate about her work that she could not manage to plan a less hectic schedule. Within a week of her departure from the Battle Creek clinic, she traveled to Des Moines, Iowa, to speak at a banquet to benefit the NAACP.

Walker inspired the audience with stories of the important accomplishments of the eight-year-old civil rights organization, but George Woodson, the local attorney who introduced her, could see that she was not in the best of health. "The eloquent force which she put into that speech in spite of her nervous state, greatly alarmed me," he wrote to Ransom. "I took her pulse in the reception room after the meeting and tried to get her away from the great mass of common people who crowded about her to admire and compliment her. But it was no use. She loved those common people and just would not leave them."

Workmen put the finishing touches on Villa Lewaro, Walker's opulent mansion in the town of Irving, on the east bank of New York's Hudson River. Walker moved into the home in 1918.

Walker thrived on knowing that her success could help other black Americans. From Des Moines, she continued a series of public appearances designed to raise money for the NAACP. "I had a crowded house and applause all through the lecture," she wrote to Ransom from Chicago as she planned stops in Indianapolis, Columbus, and Pittsburgh. "I would have to wait for them three minutes to get quiet before I could begin again. I have packed houses everywhere I have gone, notwithstanding the downpour snow."

Meanwhile, Walker's new home in Irvington was almost ready for her to move in. By the late spring of 1918, she had finished much of the decorating, spending freely in her effort to create a breathtaking environment for herself, her daughter, her granddaughter, and her many friends.

Walker lined the walls of the living room with handmade tapestries and filled curio cabinets with bronze and ivory statuettes collected from her travels. For her dining room, she commissioned hand-painted ceilings and installed recessed lighting to create a relaxed atmosphere for her dinner guests. Her wood-paneled library was stocked with works by great American authors from poet Paul Laurence Dunbar to Mark Twain, along with rare leather-bound books and illustrated encyclopedias from all over the world.

The music salon contained not only a grand piano trimmed in 24-carat gold leaf but also an organ whose music was piped through the entire house. From the first floor, a broad, curved marble staircase led to the second-floor bedrooms and sleeping porches. From the windows of her master suite, Walker could see the stone cliffs of the New Jersey Palisades across the Hudson River. The view was slightly reminiscent of the Vicksburg bluffs of her youth, which made the comparison between her early life and her present circumstances all the more striking.

The *New York Times* called Walker's new home a "wonder house," with "a degree of elegance and extravagance that a princess might envy." After describing the interior and the gardens, the newspaper noted that "the garage [has] apartments for the chauffeur and gardener. Mme. Walker maintains four automobiles. . . . She is content to let her chauffeur drive the big cars. She has, however, a small electric coupe, which she drives herself on shopping tours."

Soon after Madam Walker moved into her luxurious residence in June 1918, she and A'Lelia invited Enrico Caruso, the era's most celebrated opera star, to visit. Learning that the Walkers had not yet named their new home—a traditional practice for estate and other large mansion owners—Caruso made a suggestion. Because the grounds and the house reminded him of the grand residences of his native Italy, he proposed that they use the first two letters from A'Lelia's names—A'Lelia Walker Robinson—and call it a villa. The idea appealed to his hostesses, who agreed to christen the house "Villa Lewaro."

The image above shows the rear of the Villa Lewaro, with a gathering in its formal garden. Reporting on Walker's mansion, the *New York Times* noted that it was "in the most exclusive part of Irvington Village."

Walker took immense pleasure in her home, telling others that she hoped it would serve as a monument that would "convince members of [my] race of the wealth of business possibilities [and] point to young Negroes what a lone woman accomplished and to inspire them to do big things."

To help look after her property, Walker sent for Mr. and Mrs. Bell, the butler and housekeeper she had employed in Indianapolis. With the Bells handling the household chores, Walker could enjoy the natural setting outside her door. "Every morning at six o'clock I am at work in the garden, pulling weeds, gathering berries and vegetables," she wrote to a friend that summer. "[You] should see me now . . . all dressed up in overalls. . . . I am a full-fledged 'farmerette.' We are putting up fruit and vegetables by the wholesale."

As she planted seedlings and pruned rosebushes, Walker seemed to be reducing the stress in her life and following her doctor's orders at last. In midsummer, however, she received a tempting invitation from the National Association of Colored Women. As the contributor who had given the largest gift toward paying off the mortgage of the Washington, D.C., home of black abolitionist Frederick Douglass, Walker had been invited to a ceremony to mark the end of the successful fundraising campaign. The meeting was to be held in Denver, the city where she had sold her first tin of Walker's Wonderful Hair Grower 13 years earlier, and Walker was too excited to refuse the invitation.

A few weeks later, at the convention, as the audience sang "Hallelujah, 'Tis Done," NACW President Mary B. Talbert held the mortgage document while Walker touched a candle flame to its edge. Watching the paper crumble to ashes in a metal bowl, the two friends shared a moment of great satisfaction. The crowd rose to applaud this old-fashioned custom of burning the mortgage of a debt-free property.

"A CONFERENCE OF INTEREST TO THE RACE"

A few weeks after the NACW convention, the National Negro Business League (NNBL) hosted a special tribute to Walker and Vertner W. Tandy, the architect who had designed both her Manhattan town house and her suburban estate. Tandy, New York State's first licensed black architect, had attended the Tuskegee Institute, where Booker T. Washington had encouraged him to study architecture. By 1917, when he began to plan Walker's home, Tandy already had designed many schools, churches, and private residences. Addressing the NNBL audience, he said, "There is one person who has contributed more to architecture for Negroes than any person or group of persons in this country and that person is . . . Madam C.J. Walker."

As Walker thanked him, she was thinking of the house-warming she had scheduled for late August to honor Emmett J. Scott, former private secretary to Booker T. Washington and a founder of the NNBL. Walker had planned her weekend gathering to celebrate Scott's recent appointment to an important government post: special assistant to the secretary of war in charge of Negro affairs.

Walker's guests included several prominent black and white civil rights leaders as well as educators, ministers, and entrepreneurs. The list of invitees ranged from political activist Ida B. Wells-Barnett and labor organizer A. Philip Randolph to Richmond, Virginia, bank president Maggie Lena Walker and *Chicago Defender* publisher Robert Sengstacke Abbott. Several white NAACP members, including Board Chairman Joel Spingarn, President Moorfield Storey, Secretary Mary White Ovington, and Vice President and Treasurer Oswald Garrison Villard—the editor of the *New York Evening Post*—were also honored guests.

"It will be a very great pleasure during all the years to come that we were the first official guests entertained at Villa Lewaro," Emmett Scott wrote to Walker a few days later. "The wonderful gathering of friends . . . was beyond compare. No

DID YOU KNOW?

Shortly after Madam Walker moved to Harlem with her daughter, A'Lelia, in 1916, she purchased four and a half acres of land for a new home north of New York City in Irvington-on-Hudson, New York, near the estates of wealthy businessmen John D. Rockefeller and Jay Gould. Designed by Vertner Tandy, a 1909 graduate of Cornell University and the first licensed black architect in New York, Villa Lewaro was named a National Historic Landmark by the National Park Service in 1976. After A'Lelia Walker's death in 1931, the house was sold to Annie E. Poth, president of the Companions of the Forest, and used as a retirement home until the 1980s. Today, Villa Lewaro is privately owned and not open to the public.

such assemblage has ever gathered at the private home of any representative of our race, I am sure."

The weekend at Villa Lewaro featured more than good food and lighthearted conversation. Walker's invitation, after all, had billed the event as "A Conference of Interest to the Race." Guests discussed serious matters such as the situation of black soldiers in Europe. Everyone had read the news from the battlefields about heroic actions by black troops, particularly those of Harlem's 369th Regiment. Popularly known as the Hell Fighters, the 369th had been in ongoing combat for more weeks than any other American regiment and had been the first Allied unit to reach Germany's Rhine River.

Everyone also had heard reports of widespread racism within the military. Walker and her friends were beginning to wonder how black soldiers would be treated when they returned to the United States. Would the nation reward their heroic efforts with improved respect? Would some white Americans continue to regard these men as second-class citizens? The group at Lewaro resolved to fight for the rights of black veterans.

As the war dragged on into 1918, the Walker women became increasingly involved in the civilian war effort. Madam Walker promoted the sale of war bonds to help pay for military equipment and joined the advisory board of the Motor Corps of America, a war-relief support group. A'Lelia helped raise funds to buy an ambulance for the Motor Corps to help transport wounded black troops.

When the war ended on November 11, 1918, Walker rejoiced. She celebrated with friends in Boston and supported Ransom's decision to allow Walker employees the day off from work at the Indianapolis factory and office. The following month, Walker joined New York Mayor John F. Hylan and other dignitaries on a boat in New York Harbor to greet the troops of the Atlantic Fleet as their ship steamed home from Europe.

As Christmas approached, Walker went into her usual pre-holiday whirl, ordering festive meals, decorating her house, and choosing gifts for her family, friends, and employees. On December 23, her fifty-first birthday, a mountain of Christmas cards competed for space with an avalanche of birthday greetings from friends and admiring strangers.

The next afternoon, Christmas Eve, Walker's holiday guests began to arrive at Villa Lewaro for an evening of caroling. Walker retired early, but at midnight she awakened everyone to wish him or her "Merry Christmas."

Early Christmas morning, the guests who had gone to church returned to find Walker waiting for them before the glowing living room fireplace, where gifts were stacked high around the Christmas tree. After presents were exchanged, Walker escorted them to the dining room, where she gave thanks for the many blessings she had received during her lifetime.

As the group dined, Reverend W. Sampson Brooks of Baltimore charmed them with stories of his European travels. May Howard Jackson, an accomplished sculptor who had studied at the prestigious Philadelphia Museum School, talked about her recent exhibition at the Corcoran Gallery in Washington, D.C. A wounded soldier who had received the Croix de Guerre, France's highest medal for heroism during combat with foreign troops, told of his wartime experiences.

As she surveyed the gathering, Walker could not help but think about the hopes that her parents, Owen and Minerva Breedlove, must have had for their Christmas-season baby five decades earlier in their little cabin in Delta, Louisiana. Surely their prayers had been answered a thousand times over: Their first freeborn child now seemed to embody the most ambitious aspirations of the nation's African Americans.

9

The Legacy

By January 1919, the Madam C.J. Walker Manufacturing Company had become one of America's most successful black-owned businesses. Sales for 1918 topped a quarter of a million dollars, or more than $3.3 million in today's dollars. With the introduction of five new products planned for the spring, Walker's accountants expected the company's income to rise even higher.

Walker's financial health was soaring, but her physical health was sinking. Her doctor, Colonel Joseph Ward, who had served as a military surgeon in France during World War I, pleaded with her once again to get more rest. Reluctantly, Walker obeyed Ward's orders to the extent that she canceled all her sales trips—but she maintained regular contact with her Indianapolis headquarters and directed long-range sales strategies.

She also was too concerned about civil rights to abandon all of her political activities. During the recently ended war,

Walker had concluded that, if black Americans were to attain their full rights as citizens, they would have to assert themselves in all aspects of national and international affairs. After the war, she paid careful attention to the peace negotiations conducted in Paris between defeated Germany and the victorious Allied nations: the United States, Great Britain, France, Italy, Japan, and 23 other powers.

Walker and many of her colleagues feared that the peace treaty negotiators would ignore the rights of black Americans as well as of Africans who lived in the colonized territories controlled by European governments. Hoping to influence the treaty makers, several black leaders—W.E.B. Du Bois and William Monroe Trotter among them—decided to hold their own

The Walker Company After Madam Walker's Death

Madam C.J. Walker's only child, Lelia Walker (who later changed her first name to A'Lelia), succeeded her mother as president of the Madam C.J. Walker Manufacturing Company after Walker died in May 1919. A'Lelia Walker had been very active as a Walker Company executive in the early days of the business and had continued to run the Harlem office and beauty salon, but she handed over day-to-day operation of the company to F.B. Ransom, the attorney and general manager her mother had hired in 1911. When A'Lelia Walker died in August 1931, her adopted daughter, Mae Walker Perry, became president. When Mae died in December 1945, she was succeeded as president by her daughter, A'Lelia Mae Perry, who died in 1976. The original Walker Company remained in business until 1985, when the right to manufacture hair-care products using the Walker name was sold to a businessman named Raymond Randolph, who now is deceased. At this time, no line of Walker hair-care products is being manufactured.

Numerous other hair-care companies that follow Madam Walker's tradition have developed product lines especially formulated for black women, and several cosmetics manufacturers continue to be inspired by Madam Walker. Among them is Nadine Thompson, the cofounder and CEO of Warm Spirit, who expected to sell more than $20 million worth of products in 2006 and who models the structure for her 20,000-person sales force on some of the same principles developed by Madam Walker a century ago.

A'Lelia Walker Robinson, who posed for this photograph around 1907, moved to New York City in 1913. Intrigued by Harlem, the city's burgeoning black community, she talked her mother into buying a house there and then turned it into a stylish residence and beauty salon.

Paris meetings. Du Bois organized a group called the Pan-African Congress. Trotter, who had founded the National Equal Rights League, held a meeting to elect delegates to his alternative Paris peace conference. Among those selected as representatives were Walker and her friend Ida Wells-Barnett. The

U.S. government, however, feared the unflattering image that might result if African-American political leaders appeared in Paris to discuss social injustice and racial discrimination in an international forum. As a result, Walker, Wells-Barnett, Trotter, and others were denied the passports they needed to travel abroad.

Disappointed but not defeated, Walker continued to speak out on behalf of black Americans who still were barred from the best jobs in factories and government offices. She was particularly emphatic about the debt she felt America owed its black veterans. "Their country called them to defend its honor on the battlefield of Europe," she wrote to a white military official, "and they have bravely, fearlessly bled and died that that honor might be maintained."

Warming to her theme, she continued, "And now they will soon be returning. To what? Does any reasonable person imagine to the old order of things? To submit to being strung up, riddled with bullets, burned at the stake? No! A thousand times no! . . . They will come back to face like men whatever is in store for them and like men defend themselves, their families, and their homes."

Walker closed her remarks with assurances that she was not advocating violence or retaliation. "Please understand that this does not mean that I wish to encourage in any way a conflict between the two races," she wrote. "My message to my people is this: Go live and conduct yourself so that you will be above the reproach of anyone—but should but one prejudiced, irrational boast infringe upon [your] rights as men—resent the insult like men."

During the first few months of 1919, Walker stayed close to home, writing letters, hosting occasional dinner parties, and enjoying Villa Lewaro. Then, in late April, her friend Jessie Robinson, the former schoolteacher who now headed the Walker operation in St. Louis, urged her to visit Missouri to help launch the new line of Walker products. Although Walker was suffering from a lingering cold, she rationalized that a visit to see Jessie—one of the St. Paul AME church members who had mentored her when she was a washerwoman—might lift her spirits and be less stressful than her sales trips usually were.

On Easter Day, a few days after she had arrived in St. Louis, Walker became seriously ill. Alarmed by a spike in her blood pressure, Jessie and her husband, C.K. Robinson, arranged for their doctor and his nurse to accompany Walker back to New York. At Walker's request, the St. Louis couple chartered a private railroad car on the era's fastest train, the 20th Century Limited. According to Walker's secretary, Violet Reynolds, other passengers expressed great curiosity about their fellow traveler. They could not quite understand how a black woman could afford to travel in first-class accommodations at a time when train travel remained racially segregated by law in many states.

As the train sped across Ohio and Pennsylvania, Walker talked about all of her unfinished business, including the girls' school she hoped to build in Africa, the office building and factory she needed in order to expand her manufacturing operations, and the housing development she had planned for the poor in Indianapolis. She also longed to travel to Europe for pleasure.

Arriving in Irvington physically weak but still spiritually strong, Walker reviewed her finances and then advised Ransom to pledge $5,000 to the NAACP's crusade against racial violence. NACW President Mary Talbert announced the gift a few days later at the NAACP's Anti-Lynching Conference at Manhattan's Carnegie Hall. The 2,500 delegates cheered for several minutes. Walker's contribution, the largest the organization had ever received, so moved the convention that one wealthy black farmer from Arkansas pledged another $1,000 on the spot. By the end of the week, an additional $3,400 had been promised in smaller donations.

Walker had been too ill to attend the conference, and now Dr. Ward had little hope that his patient would recover. Her elevated blood pressure, he informed her, had hopelessly damaged her kidneys. Difficult as it was to admit, Walker knew the time had come for Ransom to draft a final revision of her will.

When he arrived, Walker presented Ransom with a list of groups she wanted to help. The *New York Age* learned that she planned to donate $25,000—or nearly $300,000 in today's dollars—to organizations and institutions that would benefit her community. "Intimate friends believe she fully realizes the seriousness of her condition," the paper revealed. "She wanted to do what she could for deserving race institutions before passing away."

Even more than her charitable contributions, Walker was concerned about A'Lelia, who was traveling in Central America on a sales trip with Mae. A letter from A'Lelia in mid-May pleased her very much, however, because A'Lelia announced that she had decided to marry Dr. Ward's protégé, Dr. James Arthur Kennedy, a surgeon who had just returned from Europe with the Croix de Guerre. Walker allowed herself to begin thinking of wedding plans at Villa Lewaro and a chance for them all to spend the summer in France.

A few days later, however, Walker's nurse reported Walker saying, "I want to live to help my race" just before she drifted into a coma. On the following Sunday morning, the *Chicago Defender* reported, the day

> dawned bright and warm. Outside, where the trees and lawn were green and pretty, the flowers blooming and the birds merrily singing, all was gaiety and happiness.
>
> Inside, where several people gathered around a beautiful four-posted bed and watched a magnificent soul go into eternity, all was grief and sorrow.
>
> Breaking the silence, [Dr. Ward] turned to those around the bedside and said, "It is over."

Fifty-one-year-old Sarah Breedlove Walker, who had transformed herself from an illiterate washerwoman into the wealthiest self-made American businesswoman of her day, had died on May 25, 1919.

Notified of her mother's death, A'Lelia struggled to find a ship in Panama that could get her to New Orleans or Miami so that she could catch a train to New York. Meanwhile, Ransom set the funeral for May 30, hoping that A'Lelia and Mae would arrive in time. Sadly, the service began without Walker's daughter and granddaughter, who were still en route to Irvington. A thousand mourners—including dozens of notable political and civil rights leaders, busloads of Walker agents, and many close friends—crowded into Villa Lewaro and spilled onto the grounds. In the music salon, Walker's pastor, Reverend James W. Brown of Mother AME Zion Church, presided as other ministers from several denominations offered tributes. Reverend William J. Brooks of St. Mark's Methodist Episcopal Church gave an especially emotional recitation of the Twenty-third Psalm, Walker's favorite Bible reading. "Farewell, farewell, a long farewell," said the minister as the service ended.

The next day, when A'Lelia and Mae arrived, they were taken to Woodlawn Cemetery to see Walker's rose-covered casket. Three days later, on June 3, Walker was buried after a small, private graveside ceremony.

Tributes continued to fill the Walker Company mailbox and newspaper columns. Walker's friend Mary McLeod Bethune called Walker's life "an unusual one." It was, said Bethune, "the clearest demonstration I know of Negro woman's ability recorded in history. She has gone, but her work still lives and shall live as an inspiration to not only her race but to the world." Writing in *The Messenger*, journalist and author George Schuyler praised Walker for giving "dignified employment to thousands of women who would otherwise have had

In 1998, Walker became the twenty-first person honored in the U.S. Postal Service's Black Heritage stamp series. The ceremony to unveil the stamp took place on January 28, 1998. Just to the right of the poster is A'Lelia Bundles.

to make their living in domestic service" as maids, servants, and laundresses.

"It is given to few persons to transform a people in a generation," W.E.B. Du Bois wrote in his obituary for *The Crisis*. "Yet this was done by the late Madam C.J. Walker. . . . [She] made and deserved a fortune and gave much of it away generously." Indeed, Walker's concern for those in need became even clearer after her death. Her will named A'Lelia as her principal heir but listed dozens of organizations and individuals as beneficiaries. She had directed Ransom to establish a $100,000 trust fund to benefit a long list of charities and left sums that ranged from $2,000 to $5,000 to institutions such as the St. Louis Colored Orphans' Home, the Home for Aged and Infirm

Colored People in Pittsburgh, the Haines Institute in Georgia, the NAACP, and the Tuskegee Institute.

At the time of her death, Walker was considered the wealthiest black woman in America and reputed to be among the first self-made American women millionaires. Her estate was valued at between $600,000 and $700,000, the equivalent of $7 million to $8 million in today's dollars. The estimated value of her company—based on annual gross receipts in 1919—easily could have been set at $1.5 million, or more than $17 million in today's dollars.

Almost a century after her death, Walker is still celebrated not only because of her financial success, but also for her entrepreneurial vision and her philanthropic generosity. In 1998, she became the twenty-first African American to be featured in the United States Postal Service's Black Heritage Series. Today, her tangible legacy is embodied by two National Historic Landmarks—the Madam Walker Theatre Center, a cultural arts center in Indianapolis, and Villa Lewaro, her Westchester County, New York, mansion—as well as by the many entrepreneurial awards that bear her name.

In 2007, Harvard Business School Professor Nancy Koehn introduced Walker's story as a case study for a course on important American entrepreneurs. Walker is one of the few women featured in the National Business Hall of Fame at Chicago's Museum of Science and Industry and frequently is cited by *BusinessWeek, Fortune, Black Enterprise,* and other business publications as being one of the most significant entrepreneurs of the twentieth century.

As a pioneer in what is now a multibillion-dollar international cosmetics industry, Walker created marketing schemes, training opportunities, and distribution strategies as innovative as those of any entrepreneur of her time. As an early advocate of women's economic independence, she provided lucrative incomes for thousands of African-American women who otherwise would have been consigned to jobs as farm laborers, washerwomen, and maids. As a philanthropist, she broadened the philosophy of charitable giving in the black community with her unprecedented contributions to the YMCA and the NAACP. As a political activist, she dreamed of organizing her sales agents to use their economic clout to protest lynching and racial injustice. As much as any of her equally pioneering female peers of the twentieth century, Walker paved the way for the profound social changes that altered women's place in American society.

1867 Walker is born Sarah Breedlove on December 23 in Delta, Louisiana.

1874 Sarah is orphaned when both her parents die within a few months of each other.

1878 Sarah moves to Vicksburg, Mississippi, with her sister, Louvenia, and younger brother, Solomon.

1882 She marries Moses McWilliams.

1885 She gives birth to a daughter, Lelia, who later changes her name to A'Lelia Walker.

1888 Sarah is widowed when McWilliams dies; moves to St. Louis with her daughter to join her older brothers and works as a washerwoman.

1903 She becomes a sales agent for Annie Malone's Poro Company.

1905 Sarah moves to Denver and develops a formula for Wonderful Hair Grower.

1906 She marries Charles Joseph Walker and changes her name to Madam C.J. Walker.

1908 Walker moves to Pittsburgh and opens Lelia College.

1910 She moves to Indianapolis and builds a factory.

1911 She pledges $1,000 to the Indianapolis YMCA building fund and establishes her reputation as a philanthropist.

1912 Walker travels throughout the United States selling products and speaking to major black organizations; she divorces C.J. Walker and becomes a grandmother when her daughter adopts Mae Bryant.

1913 She travels to the Caribbean and Central America on a sales trip.

1916 She moves to Harlem in New York City.

1917 Walker convenes the first annual Madam C.J. Walker Hair Culturists Union of America Convention; she visits the White House to urge President Woodrow Wilson to make lynching a federal crime.

1918 Walker moves into Villa Lewaro, a Hudson River mansion.

1919 Walker contributes large sums to the NAACP antilynching fund and other causes; she dies on May 25 at Villa Lewaro; she is called a millionaire because the value of her estate and her company exceeds $1 million.

1998 Walker becomes the twenty-first person honored in the U.S. Postal Service's Black Heritage stamp series.

Further Reading

Bundles, A'Lelia. *On Her Own Ground: The Life and Times of Madam C.J. Walker.* New York: Scribner, 2001.

Gatewood, William, Jr. *Slave and Freeman: The Autobiography of George L. Knox.* Lexington: University of Kentucky Press, 1979.

Giddings, Paula. *When and Where I Enter.* New York: William Morrow, 1984.

Hine, Darlene Clark, ed. *Black Women in America.* Second edition. New York: Oxford University Press, 2005.

Huggins, Nathan. *The Harlem Renaissance.* London: Oxford University Press, 1971.

Jones, Jacqueline. *Labor of Love, Labor of Sorrow.* New York: Basic Books, 1985.

Knox, George L. *Slave and Freeman: The Autobiography of George L. Knox.* Edited by Willard B. Gatewood. Lexington, Ky.: University Press of Kentucky, 1979.

Lewis, David Levering. *When Harlem Was in Vogue.* New York: Knopf, 1981.

Logan, Rayford W., and Michael Winston. *Dictionary of American Negro Biography.* New York: W.W. Norton, 1982.

Painter, Nell Irvin. *Exodusters: Black Migration to Kansas After Reconstruction.* New York: Knopf, 1977.

Peiss, Kathy. *Hope in a Jar: The Making of America's Beauty Culture.* New York: Metropolitan Books, 1998.

Roberts, Cokie. *We Are Our Mothers' Daughters.* New York: William Morrow, 1998.

Rooks, Noliwe M. *Hair Raising: Beauty, Culture and African American Women.* New Brunswick, N.J.: Rutgers University Press, 1996.

Wells-Barnett, Ida B. *Crusade for Justice: The Autobiography of Ida B. Wells.* Edited by Alfreda M. Duster. Chicago: University of Chicago Press, 1970.

WEB SITES

Indiana Historical Society
www.indianahistory.org

"Madam C.J. Walker: The Official Website"
www.madamcjwalker.com

Madam Walker Theatre Center in Indianapolis
www.walkertheatre.com

"Two American Entrepreneurs: Madam C.J. Walker and J.C. Penney,"
  Teaching with Historic Places Lesson Plans
http://www.nps.gov/nr/twhp/wwwlps/lessons/walker/walker.htm

VIDEO

"Beauty in a Jar, Production Credits," Orchard Films
Available online. http://www.orchardfilms.com/beautydetail.htm.

"Two Dollars and a Dream," Firelight Media
Available online. URL: www.firelightmedia.org/

Picture Credits

PAGE

2: The Walker Collection of A'Lelia Bundles

4: The Walker Collection of A'Lelia Bundles

7: The Walker Collection of A'Lelia Bundles

10: The Walker Collection of A'Lelia Bundles

12: Library of Congress, pga 01871

22: The Walker Collection of A'Lelia Bundles

27: The Walker Collection of A'Lelia Bundles

31: The Walker Collection of A'Lelia Bundles

35: The Walker Collection of A'Lelia Bundles

37: The Walker Collection of A'Lelia Bundles

40: The Walker Collection of A'Lelia Bundles

43: The Walker Collection of A'Lelia Bundles

49: The Walker Collection of A'Lelia Bundles

54: The Walker Collection of A'Lelia Bundles

55: The Walker Collection of A'Lelia Bundles

59: The Walker Collection of A'Lelia Bundles

66: The Walker Collection of A'Lelia Bundles

71: The Granger Collection, New York

77: The Walker Collection of A'Lelia Bundles

79: The Walker Collection of A'Lelia Bundles

86: The Walker Collection of A'Lelia Bundles

91: The Walker Collection of A'Lelia Bundles

Index

A'Lelia Bundles, Madam C.J. Walker's great-great-granddaughter, is the author of *On Her Own Ground: The Life and Times of Madam C.J. Walker* (Scribner, 2001). Her bylines have appeared in the *New York Times Book Review*; *O, The Oprah Magazine*; *Parade*; and *Essence*. A former Emmy Award–winning NBC News producer and ABC News producer and executive, she continues the Walker legacy as a member of several nonprofit boards, including the Madam Walker Theatre Center in Indianapolis, the Radcliffe Institute for Advanced Study at Harvard University, the Foundation for the National Archives, and the Columbia University Board of Trustees. She spearheaded the campaign for the 1998 Walker postage stamp and frequently gives speeches about Madam Walker. She lives in Washington, D.C.